Politico's guide to

local
government

Andrew Stevens

POLITICO'S

First published in Great Britain 2003 by
Politico's Publishing, an imprint of
Methuen Publishing Limited
215 Vauxhall Bridge Road
London SW1V 1EJ

3 5 7 9 10 8 6 4 2

A CIP catalogue record for this book is available from the British Library.

ISBN 1 84275 032 1

Printed and bound in Great Britain by St Edmundsbury Press, Suffolk.

Contents

Introduction

We look at 'World Cities' such as London, New York, Paris and Tokyo in admiration, with many quite often unaware (or uninterested, more to the point) that it is City governments that make them what they are. Former US Congressman Tip O'Neill may have coined the phrase "All politics is local", but British politics, exists in what often amounts to a very insular and enclosed world. Although of interest to what now seems like a dwindling number of people up and down the country, the main actors on the political stage in Britain manage to co-exist within a few square miles of central London. From the lobbying firm based a stone's throw away from Parliament Square and the studios of the BBC situated on Millbank SW1 through to the think tanks and advocacy organisations found in London N1, the business of politics in this country largely takes place in what often amounts to a 'Westminster Village'.

In the US, while the Presidency has *The West Wing*, local government New York-style has to make do with the sitcom *Spin City*. Therefore it should come as no surprise that local government is often seen as a poorer relation as a political institution and it certainly comes nowhere close in comparison to the 'sexiness' of national politics. The scope for surprise here is furthermore limited by the lack of power found in Councils and the roles they exercise. In terms of political careers, local government has long been seen as a convenient 'stepping stone' into Westminster – Herbert Morrison, Nye Bevan, John Major and David Blunkett all started out as local

1

Councillors before finding their way into the Parliament and ultimately the Cabinet. When Tory Foreign Secretary Malcolm Rifkind faced his Labour shadow Robin Cook in the Commons over the Scott Report, they were merely replicating the more domestic roles they had undertaken as Edinburgh City Councillors. Many political science graduates make their way to London in the hope of working in Parliament, hoping some of the Westminster 'glamour' will rub off onto them as they relentlessly photocopy Order Papers and answer letters about constituents' problems.

Outside of administrative and limited policy roles, careers in local government have been traditionally limited to specialists such as town planners, civil engineers and lawyers.

Writing about a subject as rapidly changing as local government is, like in so many other subjects in the political field, like trying to aim at an ever-moving target. But from the small Parish Council of St Osyth in Essex (pop. 4,000) to the mini-regional Kent County Council (pop. 1.3m), local government affects all of our lives in many ways, in the spheres of education, health, transport, planning, leisure and housing to name but a few.

The responsibilities of these authorities – from mineral use planning to libraries and museums – vary incredibly according to what part of the country you live in. For instance, the Geordie in Gateshead or the Brummie in Walsall has only one tier of local government to turn to for his or her local services, whereas the Kentish man or the Devonian could have three separate tiers involving a Town Council, a District Council and a County Council taking care of them. People often refer to 'the Council' in relation to service issues – "The Council is coming round to fix the drains" etc – without realising that 'the Council' is the collective body of elected members (Councillors) sitting as political representatives in committee or full Council whereas it is the 'local authority' as a corporate body that employs (or regulates) the workers who directly provide the services (although the sight of 60 or so elected members turning up to mend a drain would be amusing nonetheless).

✗ Local government is concerned with the very idea of local democracy in action. The 'City states' of Ancient Greece can be seen as the genesis of a more over-arching form of self-government, even if representative local democracy in Britain did not arrive until the mid-nineteenth century. Around that time, the liberal philosopher John Stuart Mill saw the arrival of a new breed of local political administrators as vital for the existence of local democracy.

As a political institution, local government has come a long way since ecclesiastical authorities governed localities in the Shires, through the patchwork of squirarchical local institutions of the eighteenth and early nineteenth centuries and municipalisation following the Industrial Revolution to the modern Councils of today. As this attests, this evolution was as much sociological as political – the needs of 19th century England demanded the extension of literacy and greater sanitation whereas the complex society of post-millennial Britain merits solutions to transport congestion and bridging the Digital Divide. Only local political institutions can carry out these tasks effectively and accountably according to local needs and circumstances.

Those working in local government – Councillors, officers, those in associated agencies – constantly perceive that local government is under threat from the centre and that its powers are constantly being cut back. The centre is generally obsessed with monitoring the performance of local government, with administrations regardless of their political hue managing to argue that local government is inefficient and a drain on scarce national resources. The public, for what their view is worth, consider local government to be remote, confusing and even irrelevant, hence the low electoral turnout in recent years. Despite these threats, local government continues to survive, under relentless pressure to modernise and reform from the centre, and against the low turnouts and indifference from those it serves.

Local government is quite adept at justifying its own existence through the various umbrella bodies which represent its interests to central government and the burgeoning array of think tanks and development agencies that have been created as part of the drive to bring it into the modern age. Many Councils are actually quite popular with the people they serve, some having a well-deserved reputation for providing quality services to their Council taxpayers. The names of other local authorities manage to fall off people's lips as bywords for inefficiency or even scandal and corruption. Considering many of its detractors regard it as irrelevant or obscure, the activities of some quarters of local government have at times stretched the patience of local electorates and provided acres of copy in tabloid newspapers in search of an easy target, much to the consternation of 'rent-a-quote' MPs and armchair ideologues.

The Labour government elected in 1997 placed the processes and services of local Councils under an increasing number of microscopes. Many Labour politicians served their political apprenticeships in the Council Chamber and during the opposition years of 1979–1997, Labour was the natural party of local government, with many areas resembling local one-party states. However, Labour has so far shown a tendency towards critically assessing what local government does and not accepting inefficiency in a way not that dissimilar to the Tories. Councils are expected to provide 'Best Value' to local citizens in the services they provide. Furthermore, local Councils must consult those same citizens on what the arrangements for governance in their area should be – a conventional Council leader (although with a new Cabinet-style system replacing the old committee system introduced in 1835) – or a directly elected Mayor. London now has an elected Mayor comparable in status with those in Paris and Berlin (though not New York, where the Mayoralty is the last word in City politics).

Certainly, if we were to sit down with a blank piece of paper and design a new system of British local government, provided those with a say could agree, it is doubtful that it would resemble what we have today. Labour's reforms, instigated so as to foster a concept of 'political leadership' in our local authorities, will alter the political dynamic of all local Councils and could go some way towards making Council leaders, indirectly or directly elected, more accessible and recognisable to local citizens. While the Labour government has begun a substantial programme of constitutional reform since coming into office in 1997 – reform of the House of Lords, the Human Rights Act, freedom of information legislation and devolution to Scotland and Wales – its local government reforms have come on the back of demand from local government itself and some of the ideas flirted with by the Tories.

Like many other areas of the constitution, the modern system of local government flows straight out of the feudal age. There was no Napoleonic or Prussian bureaucratic regime to bring it into existence in an ordered way and under our unwritten constitution its affairs continue to be governed by legislation passed in Parliament, as opposed to the Council Chamber. Unlike local authorities in continental Europe, its activities are governed on the principle that local authorities can only do what they are required ('duties') or permitted ('powers') to do by law and it is more affected by the doctrine of the 'Sovereignty of Parliament' as any other area of our constitution.

Indeed, for many years our local government underwent more reform, reorganisation and modernisation at the behest of central government than any other sphere of government in this country. After a century and a half of constant reform and reorganisation, Britain's local government remains subject to constant reform, with a lack of coherent arrangements requiring even more modernisation so that local government actually makes sense to people. Local political leaders will no longer be the faceless front for the majority party group on the Council; a visible leader such as an elected Mayor will be a well-known figure in their community. It is more than likely that in 15, perhaps even 10 years time local government in England will be unitary, with each area covered by only one Council rather than Shires and Boroughs.

Local government is often seen, quite often deservedly, as being a dry, boring or even pointless feature of our national democratic infrastructure. Aside from the more well-known instances of corruption and scandal in City Councils such as the T. Dan Smith era in Newcastle City Council in the 1960s or the more recent example of Doncaster Borough Council and its synonymous association with corruption, the idea of pot-boiler sensationalism in local government is the stuff of Monty Python sketches or even more recent comedy programmes. That notwithstanding, the perception of local government as the domain of superannuated party activists and the blue rinse brigade is not as accurate as many think: local government has witnessed protest and insurrection (Poplar), scandal (Portergate) and intrigue (Poulson). But the last decade has seen enough change and reform to merit the claim that local government is at last entering what could be described as an 'interesting era'.

1   A potted history of local government

> *We cannot realise the full benefit of democratic government*
> *unless we begin by the admission that all problems are not*
> *central problems, and that the results of problems not central in*
> *their incidence require decision at the place, and by the persons,*
> *where and by whom the incidence is most deeply felt.*[1]
>
> Harold J.Laski

As an Alderman in Fulham during the 1930s, Professor Laski was well positioned to understand and demonstrate the need for local government. By that time, British local government was a settled feature of our constitutional architecture and as an agency of the state was fulfilling many of the functions required by central government to ameliorate the social problems of that era[2]. The evolution of local government represents a journey through British social history in the nineteenth and twentieth centuries and its function and nature represents this as such. Of course, this was all a far cry from the time following the Norman Conquest when towns were granted Royal Charters to bestow legitimacy upon the existence of the local corporations of Aldermen and Magistrates that governed the locality through administrative and judicial supervision with local Crown-appointed Justices of the Peace carrying out this function in the Shires.

Many of these towns had boundaries and names that date back to Anglo-Saxon times. Indeed, the term the 'Hundred' came to be used as the administrative unit of that period until the medieval time.

Although retained for some purposes, the 'Hundred' then became the 'Parish' and this has remained as the parochial unit for local administration until this day. The Parish outlived the 'Manor', introduced after the Norman Conquest to administer the feudal system, and accumulated powers passed down to it by the early Parliaments, although the ecclesiastical element of its nature with which it is usually associated has diminished in the sphere of civil governance during the passage of time. The granting of lands by the monarch entailed duties upon their recipients, the noblemen and ecclesiastical figures of that age, and from this arose the array of figures of authority whose names still reflect office-holders today, archaic or otherwise, such as the Sheriff and the Magistrate.

The theory of the state that prevailed throughout this period dictated that if there were sufficient means for the collection of taxes to fund the 'defence of the realm', keep the 'King's Peace' and maintain the 'King's Highways' then there was little need for any degree of elected government beyond that at the local level. In fact, statecraft remained in its infancy and the limited forms of local governance were based on expediency rather than any kind of political need, this being the age of the curia regis where the monarch and his advisers ruled by edict and where the 'liberties of the subject' entailed a small state and the freedom to do anything the law didn't forbid. As such, local custom and circumstance could be as binding as statute. In rural and largely agrarian society this theory held sway for many years, with the enfranchised populations of large urban centres known as Boroughs electing their Members of Parliament alongside those in the rural Shires known as Counties.

Condemned by logic but approved by experience

The need for a comprehensive system of local authorities arose alongside the expansion in the population of urban centres around the time of the Industrial Revolution, with the old administrative units of what constituted the local state unable to cope with the demands placed on them, such as disease, sanitation problems, squalor and unemployment. But until this juncture, the British local state survived in its compact and limited form of feudal administrative and judicial governance under the 'Squirarchy' of the local magistracy in the rural Shire Counties and the unelected corporations of Aldermen in the Boroughs.

Like the features of the French system of government, such as Gendarmes and Prefects, many of the local institutions and officeholders of English local government survive to this day, if in name only. To understand the role and nature of local government during the feudal era, some consideration should be given to how the administrative units worked in the Shire Counties and the urban Boroughs. As part of our national constitutional architecture, the celebrated constitutional theoretician Walter Bagehot refers to local authorities as "props and fulcrums" of the Crown locally and summarises the nature of their legitimacy in his *The English Constitution*: "In the early Parliaments it was the local bodies who sent members to Parliament, the Counties, and the Boroughs; and in that way, and because of their free life, the Parliament was free too. If active real bodies had not sent the representatives, they would have been powerless. This is very much the reason why our old rights of suffrage were so various; the Government let whatever people happened to be the strongest in each town choose the members."[3]

Local Councils were, ostensibly, local electoral colleges for the selection of Members of Parliament therefore. On several occasions, monarchs tried to interfere in the local authorities in order to control the membership of Parliament. The Test Act and the Corporation Act restricted membership in the Boroughs to members of the Church of England. James II granted new Charters to some Boroughs that narrowed the franchise for elected Members of Parliament.

Local authorities existed in a very real legal sense, but they were not the only units of government. In many cases, voluntary associations and commercial concerns would exercise some of the duties required to manage the local administration of a range of duties such as poor relief and the stewardship of common lands. Eventually this diverse range of local bodies became more coherently organised along the lines of the Parishes, Boroughs and Shire Counties that would be familiar to most of us today. Generally the Parish was responsible for administrating law and order within its boundaries by appointing a Constable, providing common amenities and administering poor relief through the Overseers of the Poor. The basis for appointing these figures varied from locality to locality, some being elected and others being appointed.

The townships (Boroughs) that had obtained a Royal Charter granting them local privileges, such as the right to own corporate property such as Town Halls or refer to themselves as a 'City', were able to regulate the affairs of their inhabitants through the collection of local taxes and the appointment of a 'bench' of Magistrates, and furthermore elect Members of Parliament (hence the usage of the term 'Rotten Boroughs'). A Royal Charter granting City status to a town was usually reserved for towns acting as an established regional base for the Church with a longstanding Cathedral sited within its boundaries. The number of cities has increased over time, with many urban conurbations now possessing city status. Cities such as Ripon and Ely have been swallowed up by larger local authorities situated around them, by virtue of their small size that makes a separate local authority solely for the purposes of preserving a city to be unviable.

In addition to the Borough Corporations, in many areas associations of craftsmen and merchants came together in Gilds (or Guilds). These bodies complemented the Chartered Corporation and for regulating local trade and commercial affairs, were able to benefit from involvement in civic life. In fact, many practices of the Guilds, such as the election of officials, thus providing representation and accountability to their members, eventually found their way into local government. In some towns, the Guild was so important that the Guildhall also served as the Town Hall and some still do so to this day. This system remains in place as the means by which the sitting Councillors of the Corporation are elected in the City of London (the famous 'square mile' around the financial district) where members of 'Livery Companies' still select Aldermen to supervise the City's resources. Despite pressure to modernise the franchise, the Corporation remains committed to the system: "It is a British system. It might seem rather odd but it does work."[4] Finally, Crown-appointed Justices of the Peace, who had the right to inspect the administration of other local bodies, maintain order and punish petty crime, oversaw the running of the Counties. Furthermore, they were solely responsible for the arrangements for the maintenance of highways and bridges.

In addition to these were the numerous bodies such as Turnpike Trusts and Improvement Commissions (in a way, the forerunners of today's Quasi Autonomous Non-Governmental Organisations, or

'Quangos' as they are more commonly known), who acting as statutory bodies in some areas were responsible for highways, water and sanitation. Many of these functions required individual Acts of Parliament to sanction the creation of a local body. It is estimated that individual towns established hundreds of Paving Commissioners and Improvement Commissioners but Acts of Parliament established 1114 Turnpike Trusts, 125 Boards of Guardians for the Poor and several hundred Drainage Boards. These institutions arose by accident rather than by design over the course of time and as such began to strain under the sufferance of roles that they were not designed for in the first place.

The fall of the Squirarchy and the rise of the Board

[To] inquire into the existing state of the Municipal Corporations and collect information respecting the defects in the constitutions.[5]

As we have seen, industrial society developed at a rapid rate and the system of limited unelected government by the Counties and Boroughs was deemed to be obsolete and incapable of dealing with the demands placed upon it. The Liberal and social reformers of the day were becoming increasingly vocal in calling for a new system of comprehensive local administration that was suitably equipped to deal with the attendant social issues that the new age brought with it. We can trace the birth of municipalised local democracy back to 1835. The Royal Commission to Inquire into the Municipal Corporations was brought into existence by virtue of the widely felt perception that the Municipal Corporations had fallen into a state of major malaise and that reform was very much long overdue and necessary.

During this period, the corollary of local authorities' actions had a wider impact in other areas of our constitution and affected the quality of life for everyone. The Commission was packed with, as Sidney and Beatrice Webb later referred to them, "eager young intellectuals of Whig opinions". This was designed to ensure that the Commission reported back with Radical proposals for reform. It found that the patchwork of local authorities in existence was archaic, inefficient and inadequate and the process of reform was begun, culminating in the 1835 Municipal Corporations Act, which sought to tidy up the arrangements for local government at large and ensure that members of local Councils were in fact directly elected. However, when implemented, in practice vast sections of the local populace were in fact automatically disenfranchised when Parish Overseers neglected to include the cottages of the poor on the Rate Books. In effect, the franchise for the selection of local representative was as narrow as before. As a result, the 178 Boroughs found themselves tied to strict spending limits through their smaller rates income. In fact, it was not until 1948 with the Representation of the People Act that the franchise for local elections was widened to include non-ratepayers such as the wives and adult dependents of the actual ratepayer in the house. With stricter rules regarding funding and audits, Councils found themselves being forced to become very cautious about spending. Legal decisions had the effect of making local authorities accountable for every penny they spent and outlawed spending outside their designated function, these measures were virtually unknown under the previous system.

The former local authorities had come to be renowned for their financial extravagance and irresponsibility. The new elections of 1836 had the effect of bringing new blood into the town halls and ushering in a new breed of local Councillor (the City of London, non-directly elected, was left alone by the legislation). The former inhabitants of Councils had been predominantly Tory and Church of England but direct elections saw the rise of the Whig non-conformist merchant classes, who took their responsibilities to ensure the careful stewardship of the Rate Fund very seriously. Furthermore, local authorities themselves lost some of their former core residual functions to newly created specialist bodies.

In 1834 the Parishes lost their responsibility for local welfare under the Poor Law Amendment Act, which created new elected Boards of Guardians based on 'unions' of Parishes. The inability of some Parishes to maintain law and order led to the creation of Borough police forces (closely modelled on the Metropolitan Police) in 1835, and in the Counties in 1839. In some areas, Radicals made gains in the local elections, only to be followed by a Tory revival. As such, the stock of the local party machine rose and national party managers began to take local elections more seriously, as the development of political parties as organisations continued apace and party loyalties hardened during the debates about the extension of the franchise. By the 1900s, local elections were seen as a useful barometer for the estimation in which voters held national parties, a psephological behaviour pattern that persists to this day.

A landmark piece of legislation in the development of English local government, the 1835 Municipal Corporations Act was a direct result of the inquiry into the state of English local government, which had reported back with negative conclusions. The Act followed the 1832 Reform Act, which had the effect of extending the franchise on a limited basis to more of the middle classes. However, the inquiry found that despite extending the franchise at the national level, locally many Boroughs were corrupt and poorly run and some such as the oft-cited Old Sarum had descended into the state of having an MP but no voters on the electoral roll whatsoever. The Municipal Corporations Act was the first in a series of 'catch all' Acts to apply best practices across all of England's 178 towns and included the provision of representative government, an extended franchise, administrative efficiency and financial probity standards. These best practices were gleaned from what were at the time regarded as 'go ahead corporations'.

The urbanisation of Britain commenced the decline of rural local government. Whereas towns had governed a smaller percentage of the national population in previous times, the clamour to live near the new sources of employment around the burgeoning manufacturing and engineering industries of the towns saw the decline of rural politics. The local government of rural communities was far from democratic, based as it was on the political norms and values of the landed gentry. However, reform in this area stalled for many years for the following reasons. The impetus to reform County government was not as acute as that in the cities and the towns, where corruption and financial extravagance had become commonplace. The main obstacle, however, was the salient fact that Parliament was dominated by rural interests, who saw no need to threaten their own local power bases and political baronies.

Similar to the preceding era, the progress of local government transpired through local variation and circumstance. The 1840s saw local Councils obtain greater powers through the provision of Local Acts of Parliament – Council-sponsored Bills enacted by the Westminster Parliament for needs and circumstances of a particular locality. The drawback of this mechanism was that if a local authority was successful in petitioning Parliament for a Bill to provide a new bridge, another Bill would be required subsequently to demolish it. However, during this era, many Councils across the United Kingdom sought to advance the cause of local improvement – securing legislative change to make specific provision for their local area. For instance, in 1846, both Newcastle-upon-Tyne and Burnley Boroughs sought to prohibit the building of new houses that did not have privies attached to them, whereas Chester and Leicester acquired the right to construct public gardens and recreation grounds.

These local legislative experiments had knock-on effects for national legislation – the original laws governing the treatment of, and prohibiting cruelty towards, animals originated from Local Acts in the Midlands. As was the spirit of the Victorian age, many Councils sought powers to regulate public morals – Liverpool led the way in regulating the pawnbrokers' trade whereas Leeds acquired powers to control brothels. Birmingham sought new powers for its local police force, beyond what were operating in other local authorities during that era. In what could be seen as the beginnings of 'civic rivalry', many Councils copied the Acts of other Councils or sought to go beyond them with their own. Nationally, this era of improvement was consolidated upon by a series of Acts that sought to apply best practices of individual local authorities and apply them to all the municipal corporations in existence through national generic local government legislation.

In spite of the reforms, the problems associated with the industrial age were increasing in their prevalence, rather than diminishing. The diseases normally associated with this era – cholera, tuberculosis etc – could not be contained by local authorities under their designated function, most towns not possessing sufficient sewerage or water-treatment facilities. The 1848 Public Health Act is a landmark in the history of local government. This was a consolidation of the best provisions of Local Acts in this area and gave Councils the power to enact sufficient measures in order to try to contain the spread of disease through their burgeoning populations. However, the scope of the Act was limited insofar as it did not apply across the whole country but only where the General Board of Health thought it should or where individual local authorities had adopted it.

Despite the best intentions of the reformers in Parliament, local government remained in a state of chaos for all its own intentions of evolving alongside the urbanisation of the nation. The unsophisticated nature of local politics, developed in a vacuum without the benefit of the Westminster experience, was reduced to an unedifying farce in many Councils with petty rivalries and squabbles taking precedence over the needs of local citizens. Thus the attentions of national reformers turned to containing local democracy in an attempt to render it more effective.

Quiescent aldermanic liberalism – the rise of municipalised local services

> *The Individualist Town Councillor will walk along the municipal pavement, lit by municipal gas and cleansed by municipal brooms with municipal water, and seeing by the municipal clock in the municipal market that he is too early to great his children coming from the municipal school hard by the County lunatic asylum and municipal hospital, will use the national telegraph system to tell them not to walk through the municipal park but to come by the municipal tramway, to meet him in the municipal reading-room, by the municipal art gallery, museum and library, where he intends to consult some of the national publications in order to prepare his next speech in the municipal town hall... 'Socialism, sir' he will say, 'don't waste the time of a practical man by your fantastic absurdities. Self-help, sir, individual self-help, that's what made our country what it is.'* [6]

Sidney Webb

If we were to sit down and design a system of local government from scratch, even in the nineteenth century it would beggar belief that anyone could have found the British system of local government to be adequate for the needs of a modern society. From 1835 onwards, the history of British local government became a legislative one. The patchwork of British local government in the nineteenth century, as we have noted, evolved alongside British society as urbanisation continued apace. Throughout this period, on top of the plethora of Commissioners and local bodies already in place, we can add Library Commissioners, Commissioners of Baths and Washhouses, Burial Boards and Inspectors of Lighting and Watching as new purposeful local bodies that sprung up according to the demands of society.

However, the considerable health disorders and sanitation problems that blighted urban life still continued to prove an insurmountable challenge for Parish-centred British local government and its antiquated workings. Although the call for reform was made as early as 1836 with Joseph Hume's County Board Bill, change was actively sought by what was termed the 'Public Health Movement', led by Benthamite Liberal Edwin Chadwick. The 1868 Royal Sanitary Commission heard many pleas for action on drainage and sanitation in English towns up and down the country. The lack of central control and direction was mentioned several times during the Commission's existence. However, both local and central government resisted Centralisation. Its advocates relied upon the evidence of widespread poverty and squalor in the towns and Cities and the ineffectual nature of local authorities to deal with the problems that manifested themselves through poor drainage and sanitation. Those against cited England's tradition of local custom and circumstance as the guiding hand in local affairs.

Following the report of the Royal Commission in 1871, centralisation came, albeit belatedly and ineffectually, through the setting up of the Local Government Board as part of the Civil Service in that year. The intention of this move towards some degree of centralised control of local government affairs was an attempt to provide some national standards for local services, the reform of local government until this point being reliant upon MPs sponsoring Bills in Parliament to consolidate observed best local practice. However, local governance in the Counties had escaped scrutiny and reform until this juncture – County government acting as the last bulwark of the Squirarchy and political power base of the aristocracy outside the royal court circles of London. Indeed, Liberal philosopher John Stuart Mill remarked at the time: "the mode of formation of these bodies is most anomalous, they being neither elected, nor, in any proper sense of the term, nominated, but holding their important functions, like the feudal lord whom they succeeded, virtually by right of their acres... The institution is the most aristocratic in principle which now remains in England; far more so than the House of Lords... It is clung to with proportionate tenacity by our aristocratic classes; but is obviously at variance with all the principles which are the foundation of representative government."[7]

The peculiarities of the Boroughs merely extended to the appointment of Aldermen – robed former (or aspiring) Councillors who were able to sit as appointed members for terms of six years. County government, on the other hand, was wholly predicated on the premise that government by unelected Magistrates was an acceptable way to do business. Despite the progress made by urban Boroughs, rural local government was widely held to be lagging behind, with all the attendant social problems and issues this brought. In Parliament, rural reform of County government was a battleground between urban Radicals and the representatives of the Squirarchy, who still held sway and who were reluctant to countenance any reforms drawn up by the Radicals who could yet control any elected local Council. County government was still based on Magistrates meeting in Quarter Sessions and an earlier Royal Commission had in 1835 recommended that County ratepayers should have some say in how their rates were spent, albeit through elected Councillors sitting alongside an ex-officio Magistracy. Reform, however, was delayed by half a century by virtue of the powerful rural lobby in Parliament.

Following the passage of the 1884 Representation of the People Act (the 'Third Reform Bill') and the enfranchisement of a greater number of working men, moves towards the creation of a wholly elected County tier of local government took legislative shape in 1886 when the Liberal government attempted to promote a Bill in Parliament that was closely modelled on the 1835 Municipal Corporations Act. Similarly, the Conservatives, divided on the issue in Parliament thanks to its large rural lobby, promoted a Bill to this end in 1888, which eventually became the 1888 Local Government Act, as with the 1835 Act a landmark in local government history as it brought into being the two-tier system of Counties and Boroughs that still exists in most areas to this day. However, for the Bill to pass, several amendments had to be inserted in order to make concessions to the Bill's detractors. Early hints of Radical devolutionary measures from central government to the new County Councils were removed altogether from the Bill. In order to prevent overlapping jurisdictions or force urban and rural representatives to have to sit together in the Council Chamber (or have to pay for each others' services), a number of County Boroughs were created in order to reflect urban/rural geography.

However, by virtue of amendments tabled to the Bill, the number of these increased significantly in order to offend as least people as possible and for all manner of peculiar local circumstances, not least ecclesiastical concerns. So a situation arose where a small County such as Rutland could have the same level of governance as a large Yorkshire 'riding' (a Norse term that has remained in use). Another facet of the original Bill, a proposal to reorder the smaller local authorities, was also dropped. However, this became a separate Act under the subsequent Liberal government, the 1894 Local Government Act, which had the effect of rationalising the plethora of boards etc and creating new Urban and Rural District Councils to replace them. It also gave explicit legal recognition in government to Parish Councils as a community-based tier of small-scale local governance. By 1899, local government in England resembled a multi-tiered system reflecting differing local circumstances but substantially more rationalised than in 1834.

Pressure to respect local civic identities had been applied in Parliament in order to raise the number of proposed County Boroughs (unitary Boroughs outside of County jurisdiction) in order to protect some of the Boroughs not considered capable of exercising this role. Therefore the qualifying population level for each Borough to attain County Borough status was raised to 50,000 local inhabitants so as to allow those Boroughs to be exempt from the jurisdiction of the new County Councils that became live local authorities in 1889. One County that became live in 1889 was the London County Council, frequently held up as an example of municipal socialism in action. Municipal socialism first became evident in the programme of the Radical Liberal Joseph Chamberlain, who as leader of Birmingham municipalised the City's gas works company in 1875 and its water supply in 1876. Leading Labour thinker G.D.H. Cole was led to remark that the ideas of municipal socialism were "based more than most Fabians cared to acknowledge on Joseph Chamberlain's".[8]

A coalition of Liberals and Fabians (a founding body of the Labour Party), known as 'Progressives', took power following the Council's inaugural elections in 1889, winning 70 of the 118 seats and began the municipalisation of London's services, including the provision of public housing, a Radical measure for the time. The LCC followed the boundaries of the Metropolitan Board of Works (created following the 'Great Stink' on the Thames) to provide sewerage in and around the City of London, and had been carved out of areas of Middlesex, Surrey and Kent. Members of the ruling group included Sidney Webb (who became chairman of the Technical Instruction Committee) and Will Crooks (chairman of the Public Control Committee), who would both go on to become prominent Labour Party figures. This managed to frighten the Conservatives, who in 1899 made provision for another Local Government Act, which had the effect of creating 28 independent Borough Councils for localities such as Holborn and Camberwell, in an attempt to restrain the influence of the Progressive-dominated LCC. The gesture ultimately backfired as many of the Boroughs such as Woolwich and Poplar fell to the control of working class Councillors.

Under the direction of Fabians such as Sidney Webb, the LCC fulfilled a municipal socialist vision of its services being run for the common good of the people, as outlined in his London Programme in the 1890s. This sought the collective monopoly provision of municipalised local services, in areas such as gas, water, docks, markets, trams, hospitals and housing. Through several Acts of Parliament it became responsible for drainage, the fire service, controls on building and, in conjunction with the Boroughs, public housing. Its municipal enterprise extended to buying out all the London tram companies, doubling the provision of parks and digging two road tunnels under the Thames. In existence between 1889 and 1965 (when it was replaced by the short-lived Greater London Council), it was dominated by the Progressives from 1889-1907, Conservatives from 1907-1934 and Labour from 1934-1965, and in particular it was notable for its extensive provision of hospital services and social housing, as has been noted. This came at the end of the incremental constitutional revolution in local government that was the nineteenth century.

However, while the ensuing period of local government history could be regarded as stable in terms of reforms driven from the centre, it was most notable for the tension between local and central government and the role of local politics in the formation of the nascent Labour Party through its control of Boroughs such as Poplar, East Ham and Woolwich during the early twentieth century.

National leaders in local government 1906-1945

[The] handmaidens of parliamentary socialism...[9]

John Gyford

Despite minor fits of experimentation previously, by the turn of the century local Councils remained perfunctory bodies concerned with the daily supervision of sanitation, drainage and highways. This notwithstanding, the state of English local government was in a tidier state that one hundred years previously, when the incoherent muddle that served as local government was unelected and completely lacking in co-ordination. In their classic text on the reforms of that era, Redlich and Hirst remarked that English local government could be described as being "condemned by logic... [but] approved by experience."[10]

The elections to School Boards and Boards of Guardians had become politically charged, whereas in the mid-nineteenth century they were merely seen as the outlet for the civic-mindedness of the middle classes. In 1902, education became the responsibility of local authorities (Poor relief passing to them in 1929). The late nineteenth and early twentieth century was notable for the advances in mental health provision, with clear local authority duties superseding the anarchic and inhumane provision for the mentally ill in the Victorian era. Furthermore, the activities of municipal socialists had not passed unnoticed and the 'Liberty and Property Defence League' sprung up to act as a bulwark against what was seen as an assault on private property by pioneering socialist Councils. This took place against a backdrop of burgeoning socialist activity, Theodore Rothstein, a Communist stalwart, opined: "We must turn the local Councils into so many forts from which to assail the Capitalist order", whereas future Labour Leader and Prime Minister Clement Attlee proclaimed that: "municipal work is part of the means of changing the basis of society from profit-making to Life". However, it was Parliament and the judiciary that was able to assuage the concerns of the liberty-conscious citizens, ruling in many instances that local authorities were acting ultra vires in their endeavours. Some Councils 'massaged' previous legislation such as the Artisans and Labourers' Dwellings Act 1868 and the Housing Act 1890 to justify their house building policies.

By 1945, local government was effectively politicised with clear partisan groupings based on party political lines and whips in the Council Chambers of most local authorities, whereas in the nineteenth century, the ethos of non-political public service characterised the dealings of most Councillors. The nineteenth century was characterised by the Tory-Whig/Conservative-Liberal duopolies in the party system, although towards the end of the century the nascent municipal socialist groupings had begun to spring up in some urban Councils. Along with the Progressive coalition in London, there were Independent groupings on many Councils and certainly Ratepayers on most. Many cities and towns gave birth to short-lived local civic groupings such as the Bristol

Citizens Party and the Southampton Independent Party. In London, the Tories organised on the LCC under the quaint epithet of the London Municipal Society, whereas in Bradford the left went under the banner of the Bradford Workers' Municipal Federation. Throughout the twentieth century it is possible to find many local and bizarre examples of the small party on the Council – with defections from the main parties by disgruntled party group members giving rise to all manner of short-lived local political endeavours.

The local elections in 1919 saw a low turnout but huge advances for Labour in urban England, including taking control of a significant number of London Boroughs and English Cities or becoming serious powerbrokers in others. The electoral advances of the Labour Party mirrored the decline of the Liberal Party nationally and the rhetoric of the 'red scare' of the Zinoviev letter was copied locally as civic-minded conservatives sought to halt the encroaching advance of local socialism. As such, the local elections of 1922 saw Labour lose many of its recently gained Council seats, like in Hackney where having taken control of the Council in 1919, Labour lost all of its seats (including that of Herbert Morrison) at the elections of 1922. The ideological debate within the Labour Party was concerned with what role local Councils should play in terms of improving the lives of their citizens.

Before he became the seventh leader of the Labour Party, George Lansbury shot to prominence as the Radical Leader of Poplar Council in East London in the 1920s. The Borough of Poplar was noted for its municipal socialist zeal, building washhouses, libraries, parks and swimming baths. 'Poplarism' took its name from when Lansbury, as Leader of Poplar Council in 1921, defied the coalition government of Lloyd George over the operation of the Poor Law benefits by refusing to pay its precept to the London County Council, resulting in the imprisonment of 30 Councillors. It is reputed that sympathetic crowds visited the jails at Holloway and Brixton and sang 'The Red Flag' and the Councillors' defiant attitude to the sovereignty of Parliament was quite clearly present in the title of their pamphlet *Guilty and Proud of It.*

The effects of 'Poplarism' became widespread as over 20 Councils resisted the cuts and refused to implement the unpopular means test for the unemployed. The actions of Labour-dominated Poor Law guardians in the urban Britain certainly had the effect of eventually repealing the Poor Law legislation and removing the Dickensian conditions of the workhouse (Tory Health Minister Neville Chamberlain was so incensed by the activities of renegade socialist Boards and inept Tory and Liberal Boards that he abolished them altogether in 1929). Some pointed to Poplarism as a means to confront the legitimacy of central government whereas others saw the Fabian approach of gradually building up the size of the local public sector by stealth as the best approach. Certainly the Labour Party's establishment at national level viewed Poplarism with nothing but disdain, conscious as ever of the need to be perceived as moderate and respectful for the rule of law.

As has been noted, this era was certainly notable for its approach to experimenting with municipal social ownership – some Labour local authorities decided to try their hand at providing health centres, electricity provision and municipal savings banks. Councils also discovered the ability to regulate the working lives of local people through contract compliance, where Councils stipulated the hours, wages and union rights of employees working for private firms that bid for Council contracts. In 1923, Poplar Council made illegal payments in unemployment benefit to dockers in the London dock strikes of that year. The Boroughs of Battersea, Bermondsey, Bethnal Green, Poplar and Woolwich refused to reduce Council workers' wages, against the wishes of Whitehall.

The Housing and Town Planning Act 1919 enabled local author-ities to build more social housing and in Labour areas this was set upon with much aplomb. The late 1920s saw Labour retake many of its earlier losses as it gained control of towns and cities once again, particularly in Yorkshire. It is at this point where we can see how local elections became a political barometer for central government, although it wasn't until 1945 that Labour saw local successes translate into a breakthrough in the national polls. The economic depression in the early 1930s placed a strain on local authorities through the extra demand for poor relief and again this saw a rise in municipal militancy, although the Poor Law system was already facing abolition.

The 1930s are quite often remembered for the ideological excesses of the age, poverty and increasing international instability, leading some political activists to flirt with communism and even fascism in a minority of cases. The pro-fascist BUF contested the 1937 LCC elections, obtaining small pockets of notable support in areas such as Bethnal Green ('Lord Haw-Haw' in fact stood as a BUF candidate). However, it was the Communists who obtained electoral success in the East End that year in Stepney, whereas the Borough of Finsbury was quickly dubbed the 'Peoples' Republic of Finsbury' for its erection of a statue of Lenin. There can be no doubt that the actions of Labour local authorities during this time did much to ameliorate the bleak and harsh conditions faced by the urban poor and went some way towards attracting more supporters to the Party, this manifesting itself in the local elections of 1937.

The Tories dominated the LCC between 1907 and 1934 and although Radicalism and innovation was largely left to the Boroughs, the Tories did embark upon an extensive building programme of housing estates in areas such as Bellingham, Downham and Mottingham in South London (arguably this dispersed the working classes out of the inner city areas and therefore had the unwitting effect of placing them into hitherto safe suburban Tory Parliamentary seats, to their cost in 1945). The building of social housing was accelerated during this period, as Councils sought to diminish the Victorian-era urban squalor that still existed in many areas. Labour also made electoral breakthroughs in cities such as Norwich and Lincoln and retook the London County Council in 1934.

The LCC in the pre-war era is synonymous with Herbert Morrison, who although serving as Minister for Transport in the 1929-31 Labour government, also found time to be a local government leader as well as a Parliamentarian. As Beatrice Webb remarked: "He is a Fabian of Fabians; a direct disciple of Sidney Webb's... the very quintessence of Fabianism in policy and outlook." The LCC deservedly obtained a reputation for being well run (Morrison was obsessed with efficiency and ethical conduct) and in 1937 Herbert Morrison's Labour Party was re-elected and increased its number of seats on a high turnout.

Post-war planning and development

> *We also forget that the area of socially-owned land is gradually rising, not as a result of direct purchase by the central State, but through the decentralised activities of other public bodies – the Forestry Commission, the New Towns, the Crown Land Commissioners, the local authorities, the National Trust, and so on. This is an excellent example of how social ownership can grow without the attendant disadvantages of state monopoly.*[11]
>
> Anthony Crosland

The Labour government elected in 1945 was in fact notable for the inclusion of three former Councillors amongst its senior Cabinet members (Attlee, Morrison and Bevan). During the vast expansion of the post-war welfare state, local government was the unsung hero as central government, under the auspices of the first Labour government to serve a full term with a large Parliamentary majority, sought to bring about a Keynesian economy and gave life to Beveridge's social policy. Written in 1942 when victory over the Axis powers was far from assured, the Beveridge Report promised a vision of society far removed from the harsh reality of pre-war Britain where the 'Five Giants' of want, squalor, disease, ignorance and idleness were commonplace during the 1920s and 1930s.

Ushering in a consensus-led era of 'Butskellite' politics, local government was to become a key agency for service provision in social democratic Britain. Furthermore, the regeneration required in the inner cities after the German bombing of the Second World War saw local authorities in a pivotal role, although the need for a quick recovery and the experience of government by regional Commissioners during the war recast the perception of local authorities and their capacity to deliver on national priorities.

Despite Labour's grandiose visions for the National Health Service, which eventually came to fruition in 1948, it was originally anticipated that universal healthcare would be a function of local authorities, which already administered a large number of hospitals. However, Bevan was convinced that a National Health Service should be run by central government through regional agencies and therefore the remaining local authority and voluntary sector hospitals would have to be brought into the fold. Morrison on the other hand, argued the opposite when he said in a Cabinet paper in response to Bevan's proposals: "It is possible to argue that almost every local government function, taken by itself, could be administered more efficiently in the technical sense under a national system, but if we wish local government to thrive – as a school of political and democratic education as well as administration – we must consider the general effect on local government of each proposal. It would be disastrous if we allowed local government to languish by whittling away its most constructive and interesting functions."[12]

However, reform of the local franchise (elections were previously the preserve of the ratepayer of the house, not all adults as per Parliamentary elections) saw Labour repeat its 1945 General Election showing as it took a healthy number of urban areas into its control. Whilst Labour's local socialist measures (municipalisation) were being carried out on the national stage (nationalisation), this saw the transfer of local functions such as gas and electricity to the boards of nationalised industries. Instead, local government saw its role develop as the provider of state education and social housing, with social services becoming more prominent as a local responsibility in the 1960s. However, while Bevan did his level best to remove local authorities' responsibilities in the sphere of health provision, he did introduce legislation that allowed local authorities not only to regulate aspects of local leisure activities but also to play a leading part in their provision, especially cultural activities such as museums.

The seemingly ceaseless flow of local government reform proposals (there was another Royal Commission sitting from 1923-1929) was temporarily halted during the war but upon the resumption of government as usual in 1945 a five-man Commission was appointed to "consider the boundaries of the local government areas in England and Wales (except London) and related questions such as the establishment of new County Boroughs". The Commission was fairly critical of the local government system as it stood and recommended an overhaul of the Counties and Boroughs to meet the government's aim of "individually and collectively effective and convenient units of local government administration".

While the 1945-1951 Labour governments were regarded as economically and socially radical, they were not known for their reforming zeal in the arena of the constitution and despite their best intentions at the start, it is not surprising that local government reform was rejected and the Commission stood down.

For all the advances made with the 1944 Education Act, Labour acted somewhat conservatively on education once in government, refusing to cave in to grassroots and intellectual pressure to introduce comprehensive schooling. Education Minister Ellen Wilkinson, generally regarded as a doyenne of the left, actually favoured the retention of grammar schools as a means of creating a 'working class elite'. The social experiment that was the New Towns was based on cultivating model communities in place of the squalor previously known by Labour supporters, although those chosen to populate them had to be respectable model families themselves. The National Assistance Act of 1946 was a landmark piece of legislation, insofar as it abolished the 'Poor Law' that had been in place since 1601.

However, one of the most striking political dividing lines between Labour and the Conservatives locally during this period, was the level of Council rents. Labour's local socialism ensured that rents were kept low for the working classes whereas the Tories sought to keep rents at market levels. The Rent Act of 1957 even resulted in riots in North London when Tory-controlled St Pancras Borough Council raised its rents in 1960. Social housing became an important element of Labour's 'Homes fit for heroes' rhetoric after the war, with the house building programmes initiated under this far exceeding the programmes of the more Radical and ambitious Councils before the war. However, this agenda was shared by the Conservatives, who upon taking power in 1951 continued the programme of demolishing pre-war slums and bombed-out areas in the inner Cities and replacing them with more modern living spaces. It should be noted, however, that the preference here was for private provision and that standards in public programmes were not as high, for instance the use of high-rise tower blocks of flats to move large areas of slum-dwellers which were to become 'slums on stilts' over the course of time and present another generation with an issue to address.

The appetite for local government reform did not remain sated for long during the post-war period and inevitably the Conservative government of Harold Macmillan, which was by now boasting that it had built more homes than the erstwhile Labour government, established two new Local Government Commissions in 1958, one for England and one for Wales, their lifetimes stretching from the Conservative government and segueing into the Labour government of Harold Wilson in 1964.

The English Commission utilised a novel approach for their examinations of the many local Councils that they surveyed. Novel insofar as the Commission examined five 'Special Review Areas' based in the provinces outside of London in which they could set the boundaries status of the Counties, which they could themselves examine and review the districts beneath them. As can be imagined, this led to a cumbersome process the opportunities for vested interests to delay reform under this system were many and the recommendations of the Commission for Wales were rejected altogether. The English Commission was wound up in 1965 when the Labour government decided to create another Royal Commission to undertake a more detailed analysis with firmer terms of reference. Furthermore, the issue of London governance remained pressing for a government ensconced in the capital and more aware of its activities than those of any other local authority save perhaps those in the provincial constituencies of non-London MPs.

By the late 1950s it was widely acknowledged that London had outgrown its nineteenth century local government institutions. Yet another Royal Commission was appointed in 1957 to look at ways of providing a tier of local government that covered the Greater London region rather than just the Inner London area that fell under the London County Council's jurisdiction. It should be noted that the LCC was, before and after the war, ostensibly a Labour institution and a successful one at that. The Commission unanimously recommended the creation of a Greater London Council, taking in Tory areas in Surrey and Kent (as was the government's intention) as well as the Essex areas of the Thames corridor and the entire County of Middlesex, with as many powers as possible passing to the Boroughs beneath it, these being reduced to 52 in number. The recommendations were acted upon in the 1963 London Government Act, although the government did amend the size of the proposed authority and created only 32 London Boroughs, with education being passed to the Boroughs other than those originally covered by the LCC (in these areas education was to be supervised by an Inner London Education Authority).

Politically this period, if often noted for its adherence to the 'social-democratic consensus' and local government, aside from a few minor skirmishes between the parties, was of no exception. However, while both main parties in Parliament agreed that local government could not continue to operate on the lines which it had for over a century, neither of them actually managed to grasp the nettle of reform to a level that displayed any real results in terms of overhauling the structure. In any case, there had been piecemeal reform as a continual process since the creation of County Councils in 1889, and the presence in Parliament of those who considered 'bread and butter issues' to be of far greater relevance ensured that reform would have wait, almost until the end of the period of consensus itself.

Local government under Wilson, Heath and Callaghan

...part of the trouble in getting good enough people to serve arises... from the fact that areas and status of local authorities are often too cramped or too small to enable a satisfactory job to be done.[13]

Throughout the 1960s, the 'social-democratic consensus' remained firmly in place and the period 1964-1979 was dominated by Labour government under leaders Wilson and James Callaghan, save for the electorate's brief flirtation with Ted Heath's 'wet' Tory government between 1970 and 1974. As we have seen, the issue of municipal reform had not disappeared and the Tories' attempts at reform had yielded nothing. In 1965 the findings of the Royal Commission on Welsh local government were ignored and the English Commission prematurely wound-up with the announcement of the Redcliffe-Maud Commission to look at local government structures in England and Wales, with a separate Wheatley Commission for Councils in Scotland, which had always remained under a separate and different system from that existing elsewhere in the United Kingdom.

During the post-war period local government remained held in high regard by the main political parties at Westminster, viewed as an essential agency for the provision of services on the ground. However, as the cracks began to appear in the national social-democratic consensus, it found its friends dwindling in number for one reason or another. In an era in which political scandal was becoming more commonplace (mirroring the rise of television and the eschewal of deference by Fleet Street), the 'Poulson affair' stands out as one of the more regrettable episodes in the Labour Party's history and certainly as the most salient example of corruption in local government during recent times. 'Poulson' derives its name from the architect John Poulson, who was involved in a number of municipal architecture commissions in the 1960s and 1970s, although none more famous than the work he undertook for T. Dan Smith's Newcastle. Smith was a charismatic local political leader whose grandiose visions for Newcastle in its era of municipal improvement included turning Newcastle into a regional power base for a devolved North-eastern government, even going so far as to build space for 124 elected members of a putative North-eastern Assembly in his Council Chamber. Smith became a cheerleader for Poulson and sought to convince other Council leaders to commission him as an architect for their own municipal building programmes, relying on corrupt practices and Masonic networks to further this.

When Poulson filed for bankruptcy in 1972, the 'crony' network of T. Dan Smith was brought down with him. The episode left a bitter taste in Labour's mouth for some time to come and certainly dented the credibility of local government's ability to manage the stewardship of resources honestly in the minds of a few. However, it should be remembered that those embroiled in the Poulson affair included not only Councillors and Council officers but also a Cabinet minister, several MPs and a host of Civil Servants and public sector employees, although it is indelibly associated with local government with no flies on the others.

During the 13 years that Labour was in opposition (at Westminster), the demand for the introduction of comprehensive secondary schools as a means to abolish selective education had gone from being a lofty egalitarian ideal to actual party policy. Grassroots opinion amongst Labour Party activists, and indeed many

Councillors, was frustrated at the lack of education reform under the Labour governments of 1945–51, especially in the area of comprehensive schooling.

A small number of local authorities (such as the LCC) did, however, proceed along the comprehensive route of schooling before Anthony Crosland as Secretary of State for Education issued Circular 10/65, which had the effect of requesting that LEAs consider moving their schools over to the comprehensive system (although his junior minister Reg Prentice, a future defector to the Tories, favoured a more mandatory approach). This approach was seen as more likely to deliver – the imposition of comprehensive schooling from the centre would be fiercely resisted by many local authorities, especially the Tory Shires. The plans faltered in many areas as Labour suffered huge losses to the Tories in 1968 in many Councils, the Tories being vehemently in favour of the retention of grammar schools.

Upon assuming her post as Tory Secretary of State for Education, Margaret Thatcher immediately rescinded Circular 10/65 but the policy was revived once Reg Prentice became Labour Education Secretary in 1974 and his 1976 Education Act was specifically enacted to deal with those LEAs that refused to countenance comprehensive education. This was, of course, rescinded in 1979 when the Tories took office once again. However, this merely served to stem the tide of grammar school conversions to comprehensives, as selective schools were now the exception rather than the rule in most areas of the country.

We have noted the Tory governments of 1951-1964 and their attempts to reform the boundaries and structures of local government. The issue was revived and given extra political weight under the Royal Commissions set up by Richard Crossman as Minister for Housing and Local Government in 1966 – the Redcliffe-Maud Commission in

England and Wales, and the Wheatley Commission in Scotland. The Commissions were given clearer terms of reference and left alone to examine the workings of the local government system, which was by now widely felt to be antiquated and of little political relevance as a result, although one could consider the Commissions' work in the context of the Wilsonian drive for modernisation at the time. The Redcliffe-Maud Commission found a number of deficiencies in the way local authorities did their business, such as:

• the boundaries of most local authorities did not correspond to those of notional communities and local identities as many urban areas had grown beyond local authority boundaries
• the scale of fragmentation of local authority jurisdictions
• the confusion as to which authority did what
• the size of the smaller authorities and their ability to be effective.

The Commission published its report in 1969, which aimed for a more rational division of responsibilities within local government and for boundaries that made more sense to the people it served. The proposals it came up with were based on the need to reconcile the interests of town and country and "strike a balance between the claims of efficiency, democracy, community and continuity".[14]

It recommended that England should be divided into 58 areas of unitary authorities (akin to the status of the County Boroughs). Three areas of England should have a two-tier system (akin to the new Greater London Council and 32 Boroughs). The Commission also recommended that two other non-operational tiers should be introduced: local Councils that could provide a minor representational role, and regional Councils to provide a strategic planning element to the proceedings. The Commission's findings received a mixed response, some proposals being more palatable than others, but Harold Wilson's Labour government accepted the report. The election of Ted Heath's Conservative government in 1970 prevented the Labour government from implementing it in any case.

The ranks of Labour Councillors are often swelled by elderly party members (an abiding trend to this day) but when many of these lost their seats in the late 1960s, many of them were too old to be re-elected in the 1970s, thus allowing a new intake of Councillors to take office. These Councillors were quite often leftwing and as such this saw a new era of local authorities challenging the wisdom of central government, regardless of its political complexion. A minor flashpoint of 1970s municipal militancy came in 1972 when Clay Cross UDC in Derbyshire refused to observe the new Housing Finance Act (obliging it to raise its rents) and, following a period of non-co-operation with the demands of central government and the Commissioner appointed to temporarily supervise the collection of Council rents, the 'Clay Cross 11' (as they have become known) were disqualified from office.

Aside from housing and the powers to ensure decent standards of hygiene and sanitation, local government was coming under pressure to take an active lead in personal social services on top of its responsibilities under the 1946 National Assistance Act. Films such as Ken Loach's *Cathy Come Home* drove this home in terms of raising public consciousness. The 1970 Local Government Social Services Act stipulated that local authorities had to create their own social services departments to take the lead in this area in their localities. However, under the National Health Service Act 1973 local authorities lost their remaining responsibilities in terms of local healthcare such as the provision of health centres and ambulances (this was finalised in 1990 when they lost their representation on health authorities altogether).

Many of the reforms proposed by Redcliffe-Maud were predicated on the need to attract a better calibre of local Councillor to local government. This agenda was furthered by the Bains committee, a working party set up to advise on management structures in local government to complement the work of Redcliffe-Maud for insertion into the legislation required. The Bains report recommended a streamlined internal management system for the new local authorities and its recommendations were largely accepted by the Heath government as they were less radical than the Redcliffe-Maud proposals and would go some way towards instilling a more 'corporate' approach to the way local authorities did business, as was the managerial approach of Heath at the time.

The Redcliffe-Maud report, parked since 1969, made its way onto the statute books and town halls across England and Wales, to some extent, in the 1972 Local Government Act. The Conservatives had faced internal opposition to the loss of County Councils and the government indicated early on that it preferred the evolutionary approach by introducing a comprehensive two-tier system of Counties and districts in the majority of England and Wales, and metropolitan Counties and metropolitan districts in six urban areas of large population density. The ostensible difference between the two types of County was that functions such as education and social services remained at County level in the Shires, whereas in the metropolitan areas they would be carried out by the districts.

The government adopted the 'big is beautiful' approach in terms of Counties, preferring large geographical units covering both town and country (the inclusion of rural areas was felt to be of electoral benefit to the Tories sitting on County Councils). The creation of the three 'artificial' Counties of Avon, Cleveland and Humberside was unpopular from the start, although the rural areas included (the source of opposition) was at the behest of Tory Environment Secretary Peter Walker in the interests of Tory representation on these largely urban Councils. However, these artificial areas moved away from the idea of what German sociologist Ferdinand Tonnies referred to as Gemeinschaft, that is a territory based on real communities; Gesellschaft, an artificial area imposed from above, will not command any degree of association with the local agencies serving the people, he argued. Furthermore, cities such as Bristol, Derby, Leicester and Norwich were reduced to the same status as other (smaller) districts – although they were permitted to retain their conferred 'City' status.[15]

On top of the 1972 reforms, the 1974 Local Government Act created the office of the Local Government Commissioners, more commonly known as Ombudsmen, to provide individual redress for local authority misadministration, an overdue measure in terms of providing a greater degree of accountability in the workings of local government. In the spirit of this new era of critically assessing the workings of local government, the Labour government created a Committee of Local Government Finance, which reported with the 'Layfield Committee Report' in 1976. This was the first in a series of attempts to control the growth of local authority expenditure. Against the backdrop of wider economic uncertainty as the era of Keynesian spending of the social-democratic consensus violently drew to a close, Labour Environment Secretary Anthony Crosland was led to remark to an audience of local Councillors: "With its usual spirit of patriotism and its tradition of service to the community's needs, [local government] is coming to realise that, for the time being at least, the party is over."[16]

The 'new urban left' and municipal socialism in the 1980s

... a more radical attitude on the part of Labour Councils has quickly turned local government into a terrain of quite fierce

conflict; and such occasions have become more frequent in recent years, given the determination of central government to cut expenditure and services. In this part of the political system as in all others, the application of greater and more forceful pressure from below produces strains and tensions which raise some very large questions for capitalist democracy.[17]

Ralph Miliband

In the late 1970s, the electoral unpopularity of the Labour government of Jim Callaghan saw the Tories take many Council seats in urban areas. However, Labour slowly crawled back to power in many Councils and the election of Margaret Thatcher in 1979, although setting the scene for a decade of conflict between the tiers of government, represented the high watermark of Tory success in local government elections.

However, a sea change in local government politics had already taken place, with the ascendant leftwing of the Labour Party taking control of many local Labour Parties (and therefore Council Labour Groups). Sensing betrayal by Wilson and Callaghan, the Left's faith in the Parliamentary Labour Party to deliver socialism was considerably dented and an 'extra-parliamentary' strategy was envisaged, with local authorities as one of the frontiers in a pitched battle against the authoritarian state, as in the 1920s with Poplarism. This went beyond the 'gas and water socialism' of the early Fabian collectivists and echoed the sentiments of the Communist Theodore Rothstein when he argued in the earlier part of the twentieth century that local Councils could be used as instruments of revolution against the central state. By the time of the "longest suicide note in history" at the 1983 General Election, the term 'loony left' was already being banded around furiously by Fleet Street and the (reported) behaviour of many Labour local authorities could only add to Labour's electoral woes.

In their Fabian Society pamphlet *Building from the Bottom: The Sheffield Experience*, David Blunkett (then Leader of Sheffield City Council) and Geoff Green helped define the agenda of the New Urban Left (as it was now less pejoratively known) when they argued that: "the concept of community can form an alternative to that of greed and self-interest".[18] Thus, Labour local authorities saw themselves as a bulwark against the individualism and 'greed-is-good' philosophy of Thatcherism. Such an aim could be seen as benign and worthwhile if viewed in this context, although many would argue that it was not something local authorities should have been concerning themselves with. However, it is worth noting that future Home Secretary Blunkett also argued that local government's role was as a "rudimentary opposition movement against the ruling party in Westminster."![19]

The agenda of the new urban left in the 1980s deviated from that of its predecessors in the 1920s as it sought to go beyond service provision and became more interested in areas such as equalities, culture and addressing deficits in the economy, particularly unemployment. The backdrop of increased Cold War anxiety, inner city riots (particularly the poor community relations profile of the police) and rising unemployment and industrial unrest gave radical Labour local authorities the opportunity to flex their muscles and rattle a few sabres at the Thatcher-led Tory government through gestures such as 'nuclear-free zones'. Indeed as Lansley, Goss and Wolmar remarked in their study of what the right termed 'loony left' Councils: "The new Councillors wanted to increase spending, to extend the role of Councils, and to use local authorities as a weapon to campaign for a variety of political causes."[20]

If organisations such as CND, trade unions such as the National Union of Mineworkers and individuals such as Peter Tatchell (as putative Labour MP for Bermondsey) exemplified the character of the 'loony left', then Labour local authorities (with one or two exceptions such as the traditional Labour redoubts of Birmingham and Newcastle) proved to be a convenient hangout for the scourge of Fleet Street, Whitehall and perhaps even Labour Party headquarters at Walworth Road. If one was to believe the more sensationalist scribblings of the tabloid press, then the daily life of an average Labour Councillor consisted of thinking up new ways to indoctrinate children into deviant lifestyles and correct our linguistic behaviour by banning 'racist' nursery rhymes such as 'Ba Ba Black Sheep' and 'sexist' terminology such as 'manholes'.

Admittedly Fleet Street hacks were picking on isolated examples of some of the more ridiculous examples of Labour Councillors' behaviour but in some cases the charge was justified when it was argued that many local authorities had become more obsessed with the wider problems of society as they saw them, than merely providing local services: "For them, providing services to people is not enough. Their commitment is to involve a wider range of the public in the process of decision-making and implementation... For them, local politics should also be about raising public concern about nuclear power and disarmament, ill-health, economic restructuring, equal opportunities and new forms of poverty."[21]

The advance of the left in the Labour Party was unfortunately associated with the existence of the Trotskyite Militant tendency, who. although usually lumped in by the media with the likes of the GLC's Ken Livingstone and London Borough Council Leaders of the time such as Linda Bellos and 'Red' Ted Knight, were, politically speaking, actually to the left of most of the new urban left.

The only local authority that Militant (taken from the name of the newspaper enthusiastically sold by its members) exerted any degree of real control in was Liverpool, where the Liberals had made some in-roads in the 1970s. Alongside 'Red' Ken Livingstone, the women of Greenham Common and miners' leader Arthur Scargill, Liverpool's Deputy Leader Derek Hatton made a convenient bogeyman for the right-wing press of the time. Liverpool, like many other urban centres during the 1980s, had suffered at the hands of de-industrialisation, with the attendant social problems. Many of its housing estates had fallen into severe neglect and combined with high levels of unemployment, it was of no surprise that Toxteth took its place alongside Brixton in the inner city riots of 1981. Liverpool had been Militant's power base outside of London since the 1950s and had come to be more influential in the city's Labour Party by the 1980s when Labour regained control of the City Council from the Liberals in 1983.

As is associated with the communist-inspired left, the role of propaganda is significantly important, as can be seen in former Militant General Secretary Peter Taafe's analysis of Militant's occupancy of Liverpool City Hall: "Since 1979 the condition and rights of working people appear to have been crushed by the Thatcher juggernaut. In reality, the working class has put up ferocious opposition to the Tory government. This reached its height in the titanic year-long miners' strike of 1984-85 and in the stand of Liverpool City Council between 1983-87."[22] The episode was more unfortunate as it came to be associated with the more unsavoury practices of intimidation of opponents, cronyism and a lack of regard for resources.

Inevitably, the Labour Party sought to impose control of the city Labour Group's affairs and by 1986 the affair was largely over. Indeed, in a famous speech of the time, Labour Leader Neil Kinnock lashed out at Hatton and co. in his 1985 speech to the Labour Conference of that year when he remarked upon: "the grotesque spectacle of a Labour Council, a Labour Council, hiring taxis to scuttle around a City handing out redundancy notices to its own workers… you can't play politics with people's jobs." As Derek Hatton left the conference hall in disgust, closely followed by left-wing firebrand Labour MP Eric Heffer, arguably the highpoint of municipal militancy was now over, with any flashes of deviation from the approved moderate party line being quelled very quickly by the centre in the battle to make Labour more respectable locally and therefore more electable nationally.

Of course, in any conflict there must be more than one party engaged in the battle and it would not do to leave the Conservative Party out of the analysis. Mrs Thatcher's New Right project was disdainful towards the role of local government and the part it played in driving up central government expenditure and it was a sure-fire target for her intentions to "roll back" the bloated and over-fed state. But by 1985, the Conservatives in local government were in retreat as Councils in unlikely places as East Sussex and Berkshire were transferred out of their control after almost a century of dominance. In the tradition of Neville Chamberlain's response to Poplarism in the 1920s, Margaret Thatcher sought to end central government's reliance on local government as the local agency for the delivery of services. Indeed, as Peter Jenkins remarked, Tory ministers "were of the opinion that reversing Britain's decline was too serious a business to be left to the sort of people who these days got themselves elected to the town and county halls." [23]

One of the measures applied by the Conservatives in order to curb excessive town hall spending was rate capping. This saw central government stipulating the maximum rate that could be set by local Councils and in many town halls Labour Councillors attempted to revolt against the measures by refusing to set a rate in a stand-off against central government. When this was ruled illegal, the number of Councils rebelling dropped considerably and by 1985 only

Liverpool and Lambeth were left battling, resulting in some Councillors being removed from office and surcharged for failing to adhere to their legal duty to set a rate. However, the rate set by Liverpool did not cover its spending commitments and following finance officers' advice that Council staff could not be paid (the local authority was the City's largest employer), the Council issued redundancy notices to its staff.

The failure of Labour local authorities to win the rate capping revolt of 1985 saw the demise of Militant on Merseyside (a leadership-led purge later removed it altogether from the Labour Party) and, as previously argued, the end of the new urban left era in local government.

Many Labour authorities had proved themselves quite adept annoying the Tory government through their extravagant spending and metropolitan liberal attitudes to education, policing and the arts. A special place in history must surely be reserved, however, for the GLC in its Ken Livingstone incarnation. Ken Livingstone, elected GLC Leader in 1981 in a coup d'etat in the GLC Labour Group, was the only GLC Leader in its 20-year history not to receive a knighthood – a telling fact in itself (although he probably wouldn't have accepted it anyway). The GLC was designed during Harold Macmillan's tenure as Prime Minister to accommodate the more Tory-inclined outer London suburbs.

The Tories' strategy was successful and the GLC was ostensibly a Tory institution throughout the bulk of its relatively short lifespan, giving London such colourful characters as Sir Horace Cutler, Livingstone's predecessor as leader. Again, the period is best known for the tabloid vilification of 'Red Ken' and his Women's Committee, anti-apartheid campaigns, Nicaraguan coffee-selling canteens, sponsorship of gay and lesbian groups and links with the IRA and PLO. It is true that Livingstone was responsible for a wider cultural and political agenda than that which the GLC's mandate actually allowed for, but most tabloid hacks were over-generous in terms of the emphasis that they thought the GLC placed on these issues.

However, Livingstone did steer the authority on a collision course with central government and quite often deliberately set out to provoke the ire of Mrs Thatcher and the rest of the Conservative Party assembled in Parliament across the Thames from County Hall. The two areas that the GLC earned its radical policy spurs in were transport and unemployment. Its 'Fare's Fair' policy of cheap public transport for Londoners was, for obvious reasons, popular with Londoners but ruled as illegal in the House of Lords. It also challenged the Tories, belief that only the free market could lower unemployment (it actually displayed the number of the capital's unemployed on the front of County Hall, which sat opposite Parliament at Westminster) by setting up the interventionist Greater London Enterprise Board (GLEB).

The Tories couldn't stomach the sight of municipal socialism in their Westminster backyard and set about abolishing the GLC, Norman Tebbitt remarking that the GLC had to go because it was: "Labour-dominated, high-spending and at odds with the government's view of the world." Thus in 1986, after only 20 years of existence, the GLC was airbrushed out of history, leaving London as the only capital city in the West not to enjoy a representative tier of government as its responsibilities were shared out between the Boroughs, the City of London Corporation, five government departments and 60 Quangos and committees.

The antics of the municipal socialists had certainly not gone unnoticed by the Tory government and it was widely felt that something should be done. In addition to the GLC, the Tories abolished the six Metropolitan County Councils that served the large cities and their surroundings in the provinces of the North and Midlands (South Yorkshire Metropolitan County Council was dubbed 'the People's Republic of South Yorkshire' throughout this time). It also created the Widdicombe Committee, whose remit was to get to grips with many of the tenets of municipal socialism. It found that 16% of local Councillors were in the employ of other local authorities, such as the case of Liverpool Deputy Leader Derek Hatton who was employed by neighbouring Knowsley Borough Council in a well-paid part-time post that enabled him to be virtually a full-time politician. Therefore it recommended in its report, *The Conduct of Local Authority Business*, that senior local government officers should be debarred from also being Councillors or even engaging in political activity.

The government implemented this in its 1989 Local Government and Housing Act. The government also inserted into its 1988 Local Government Act provisions to prevent schoolteachers from seeking to "intentionally promote homosexuality or publish material with the intention of promoting homosexuality" or "promote the teaching in any maintained school of the acceptability of homosexuality as a pretended family relationship" (this became notoriously known as Section 28).[24] The Act was largely concerned with encouraging local authorities to outsource their services but the inclusion of Section 28 came about through the Tories' perception that 'politically-correct' teachers were seeking to teach children that homosexual relationships were equally as valid as heterosexual ones, as a result of children's books such as Janet lives with Peter and John. The measure was one of the more controversial 'reforms' instigated by the Tories and no prosecution has ever taken place under it.

The Conservatives also created Urban Development Corporations (UDCs) in several urban areas. These Quangos had a 15-year mission to regenerate inner city communities by market-led

approaches and owed their powers to those taken from local authorities (particularly planning), although their secondary purpose was
to install vestiges of middle-class life into urban areas (luxury apart-
ments, yachting marinas etc) for partisan reasons, especially when
considered alongside the non-LEA selective City Technology
Colleges that were sometimes built nearby. The UDCs were a costly
exercise and many have pointed to how the funds could have been
better spent by democratically elected local authorities, as many of
the grandiose schemes they instigated were as frivolous as anything
put forward by local Councils during this period. However, they,
along with City Technology Colleges, demonstrated the Tories' wish
to see the local state cut back even further and the role of local businesses increased in the provision of local services.

Education was another area of radical change by the
Conservatives during this period. The reforms of Kenneth Baker in
this area with the 1988 Education Reform Act altered the post-war
consensus on the role of LEAs in the provision of education. In the
name of increasing choice (arguably many LEAs had begun to
approach education as a purely bureaucratic exercise), the Tories set
about allowing schools to opt of LEA control, introduced a
National Curriculum, reformed school governing bodies to make
them more accountable for budgets and removed polytechnics
from LEAs altogether. This was packaged as allowing for schools to
exercise a greater degree of self-government but critics saw it as an
exercise in centralisation. During this period we became acquainted
with the 'Tory flagship' Councils such as Wandsworth, who in the
1980s showed the rest of local government how to behave like
model local Thatcherites. One of these Councils (another London
Borough) was the Westminster City Council of Dame Shirley
Porter. Dame Shirley is now better known for her role in the
'homes for votes' scandal that engulfed Westminster City Council

in the 1990s when it was revealed that homes had been sold in marginal Tory wards for partisan advantage during the 1980s, to the cost of £21m.

As a former Labour Councillor during the heady days of the new urban left in the London Borough of Islington, Spectator columnist Leo McKinistry was led to bitterly argue in 1995 that: "For me the two most repugnant features of socialism in practice – as demonstrated by the Labour Party and its swathe of local authorities – are its political correctness and its belief that government spending is the solution to every problem."[25] The Local Government Act of 1988 largely put paid to both of these. Firstly, as we have seen, the inclusion of Section 28 drew a line in the sand for the bounds of local authority 'political correctness'. Secondly, the Act was also concerned with the introduction of Compulsory Competitive Tendering (CCT). CCT was an attempt to maximise private sector involvement in the provision of local services on one hand, and a desire to make existing local authority service departments more efficient on the other.

The Tories were frustrated that Labour authorities did not share the zeal or even the inclination to subject their services to competitive tendering as Tory Councils such as Wandsworth did. Instead, Labour Councils cited social considerations for keeping their services in-house. Tory Environment Secretary Nicholas Ridley wanted to transform local government from its role as a service provider to merely an 'enabling' body that met merely to dole out contracts for local services to the private sector. CCT was phased into existence gradually to allow for the compulsory outsourcing of local authority cleaning, maintenance and catering services (1988), sports and leisure facilities (1989) and financial and technical services (1992). Local authority Direct Service Organisations (DSOs) now had to compete alongside private firms for local authority contracts. This was arguably the zenith of the New Right project for local government.

Local government reform in the 1990s – the Major years

> ... *if it really is true that the recent local government reforms are working as badly as I have heard it suggested, it may very well be that a revision of boundaries and functions, if found necessary, could be better done by locally elected assemblies than by Parliament operating through the large ministries in Whitehall and driving through the reformed arrangements by guillotine on a pattern wholly uniform throughout the country.*[26]

Lord Hailsham

The last major local government reform of Margaret Thatcher's Conservative administration was as concerned with financial efficiency as any of her others. It would also prove to be a tragic mistake even by the Tories' own admission. The Thatcher government was determined to curb what it perceived to be the excesses of the local state and had year on year enacted at least one Local Government Act throughout the 1980s and transferred a number of key responsibilities (higher education, urban renewal) to Quangos. Furthermore it was determined to make local authorities more accountable for their spending and to instil a 'client culture' into service provision. Compulsory Competitive Tendering and rate capping could only go so far in achieving this and the Community Charge (the so-called 'Poll Tax') was packaged as the means to achieve greater accountability for local authority spending and the final step change towards a client/service provider relationship by abolishing the rates system.

Pushed through in 1988, despite considerable internal opposition within the Conservative Party, the Poll Tax was a flat rate levy (regardless of ability to pay), payable by all adult residents in a local authority area. However, opposition to the tax was immense, not least from the general public (manifesting itself in mass non-payment and the Poll Tax riots in London in 1990) but also local government itself (several Labour Councillors even went to prison for refusal to pay). By 1990, Margaret Thatcher was gone from 10 Downing Street and her successor John Major resolved to replace it. Thatcher's challenger to the Tory leadership, Michael Heseltine, was appointed Environment Secretary in John Major's first government and charged with finding a replacement. After considerable debate, Heseltine proposed the Council Tax (based on property values as opposed to individuals), which remains in place today.

Aside from abolishing the Poll Tax, one of the Michael Heseltine's first actions as Environment Secretary was to consult on the boundaries for new unitary authorities, as the government was keen to oversee more reform and a reduction in the number of local authorities. Throughout the 1980s, the relationship between central and local government was marked by tension over the transferral of local government's powers and responsibilities to unelected Quangos and John Major's government proved no exception to this. In 1973 the Heath government took away the last remaining responsibilities of local authorities in the sphere of health services. With the National Health Service and Community Care Act of 1990 the Major government stripped away the final vestiges of influence that local authorities might have had in this area by removing them from the boards of health authorities.

Under the Local Government Act 1992, the government established a Local Government Commission, headed by Sir John Banham, to examine the possibilities for reform of the local government structure in England (there were separate Commissions for Scotland and Wales) in order to bring about unitary local authorities across Britain. The Commission held a series of inquiries and deliberated at length (1992-1995) and was charged with recommending the most acceptable proposals for unitary authorities across the country. The government's preference was for single-tier all-purpose unitary authorities throughout the country (akin to the Metropolitan and London Boroughs since 1986), ending the two-tier system created in 1974. It believed that these would be more efficient, focused and coherent and would end duplication of provision and confusion amongst the public. However, this was not what the Commission ended up recommending, as we will see later.

There was more 'reform' with the Further and Higher Education Act 1992, which removed local authority Further Education and Sixth Form Colleges from LEA control and placed the new 'Further Education Corporations' (the independent corporate bodies administering each individual college) under the watchful eye of Whitehall and its Further Education Funding Council (a similar body was also established to fund the former LEA polytechnics taken out of LEA control in 1988). It was argued that this would lead to more choice for students in terms of the ability to vary and extend the courses on offer locally, and a more 'business-like' approach in terms of running the corporations would lead to greater efficiency than was the case under LEA control. The extension of choice in education was the rationale behind the 1993 Education Act, which also extended the provisions of the 1988 Education Act and allowed more schools to opt out of local authority control into Grant Maintained status. Again, critics saw this as the erosion of local democratic control of schools and a further extension of the Quango state begun with the creation of UDCs and TECs. The increasing number of Councils in the hands of Labour were suspicious and disdainful of these bodies, many without local authority representation, and set up 'Quango committees' to monitor them. Other 'reforms' of the era saw local authority representation on police authorities halved and the privatisation of the local authority careers service.

Local Government Reorganisation is the main legacy of the Major years as far as local government is concerned. The government's preference for unitary authorities was clear, but so was the preference of the status quo by local government itself. In Scotland and Wales, where the lack of Tory MPs exerting pressure for the retention of County Councils was minimal, the task of recommending a system of unitary authorities was far simpler than in England. Scotland's nine regional and 53 district Councils were scrapped in favour of 32 new unitary Councils, which came into existence in 1995. In Wales, the number of Councils went down from eight Counties and 37 districts to just 22 unitary authorities.

In both countries, the government's plans were met with stern opposition, from trade unions, the Labour Party and of course, local government itself. However, the new system was pushed through easily enough. In England it was an altogether different story. Despite the PR campaigns they mounted (admittedly not as flashy as that of the GLC in its final days), the 'unloved' artificial Counties of Avon, Cleveland and Humberside were brushed aside with a stroke of the legislative pen after only 22 years in existence. The Commission had a far harder task in finding acceptable proposals for the other Counties it had to consider. On paper, the exercise consisted of deciding which districts or Counties could take over all local government in their area and where new authorities would have to be carved out on the map.

However, in seeking to find a balance between what already existed and the new desired unitary authorities, conflict of opinion was inevitable as to define boundaries that are smaller than a County but larger than a district entails both tiers losing out. In particular it was difficult to create viable unitary authorities in rural areas. The result was, unlike in Scotland and Wales, a dog's breakfast in terms of the hybrid system offered in England. There was to be no comprehensive single-tier layer of unitary local authorities. In some areas the Counties and districts were retained, but in most cases the new unitary authorities (such as Peterborough and York) sat like islands in the middle of two-tier Counties. With the loss of Avon, Cleveland and Humberside came the return of Herefordshire, Rutland and the East Riding of Yorkshire (absent as Counties since the 1960s and 1970s but restored as unitary authorities).

However, the exercise was largely seen by many as a flop in terms of not delivering upon its terms of reference to recommend a comprehensive set of unitary local authority boundaries across Britain. The workings of the Commission were subject to the intervention of more than one Cabinet minister and by the end of the process the government had lost its initial enthusiasm for reform. This was acute in the light of hostile public opinion (against well-known Council areas "disappearing off the map") and Tory rural backbenchers defending the interests of County Councils, all of this taking place at a time when the government was sliding in the opinion polls and dependent on a wafer-thin Parliamentary majority.

The local elections of May 1995 were something of a high watermark for the Labour Party in terms of electoral showing, the poll being, in effect, a plebiscite on the Major government's performance. Following the honeymoon period after Tony Blair's ascendancy to the Labour leadership, it was widely anticipated that Labour would win the subsequent general election and work was already in train on formulating policies for government. In particular, the Labour Party was forging a radical constitutional agenda, including the devolution of power to Scotland, Wales and the English regions and as such was seeking consensus on devolution.

The Commission for Local Democracy played a minor part in that process, although its creation was at the behest of local government in order to stimulate a debate around the future role of local authorities following tension between the centre and local government and the Tories' 'rolling back' of the local state. Its report, *Taking Charge: the Rebirth of Local Democracy* (1995), was influential on some aspects of future local government thinking such as elected Mayors, as we will see in later chapters.

2   National and regional variations

London

As the national legislature and seat of government are based in the capital, London's local government has always received an unwarranted degree of attention from national politicians. As such, the role and form of local government in London have largely differed from the rest of the country. London was certainly exposed to a greater degree of rapid urban growth (and therefore societal pressures) during the nineteenth century and this explains this pattern of political behaviour. Until the nineteenth century, London was largely taken to mean the City of London (the area around the historic 'square mile' governed by the Corporation of London) and perhaps the assortment of Boroughs surrounding it such as Southwark and Westminster (a city). Seemingly as London 'expanded' throughout Essex, Kent, Middlesex and Surrey, each year would see another ad hoc board tacked on to the plethora' that already existed and were failing to cope with the increased demand for local services.

London was not covered by the reforms of 1835, the City of London Corporation having mounted a successful lobbying exercise against the extension of reform to within its boundaries. To tackle the wider problems of London governance would be to question the unelected nature of the City Corporation and it remained untouched for another 20 years. The 'great stink' of 1858 spurred MPs into action as the lack of decent sanitation in London was affecting the Houses of Parliament. Even then, the ensuing legislation was a compromise – the Royal Commission appointed on this occasion was of the firm belief that the unique circumstances of London merited a different approach and that a single all-purpose elected Council would not be appropriate.

The Metropolis Local Management Act of 1855 had created 99 parish areas, the bulk of these being grouped into districts supervised by a District Board, that were responsible for the basic services such as drainage, paving and street cleaning. Above these was the Metropolitan Board of Works; its 45 members were nominated from each of the District Boards, which was responsible for the supervision of major sanitation in the capital. Over time it accumulated more powers so that it could exercise some responsibility for housing, road improvements and the fire service.

As would be expected though, this was far from ideal. The incoherent pattern of government did not give rise to efficient services and furthermore, because of its unelected status, the Metropolitan Board of Works was lacking in legitimacy. The government's predilection for appointing ad hoc bodies in the capital continued unabated, such as the London School Board and the Metropolitan Asylums Board. The mere fact that local government in other parts of England was being reformed and reorganised had not gone unnoticed and allegations of corruption in the Metropolitan Board of Works gave rise to a small movement for change in the capital. A coalition of groups such as the London Municipal Reform League and the Fabian socialists were part of the movement that led to the creation of the London County Council in 1889 as a result of the 1888 Local Government Act that created County Councils alongside it in other parts of England.

However, the trend of appointing more administrative bodies outside the remit of the elected tier of government continued – the Metropolitan Police, Burial Boards and the grandly named Thames Conservancy Board. The LCC quickly developed into an eminent institution in the capital. The first administration was a 'Progressive' coalition of Liberals and Fabian socialists, the latter envisaging the LCC as a body to co-ordinate municipal socialist enterprise in the capital (such as the municipalisation of gas, water, transport and docks) and wider social programmes in housing and unemployment. This duly alarmed the Conservative government of the time, who produced the 1899 Local Government Act, which sought to introduce a lower elected tier of 28 Boroughs to replace the plethora of boards and vestries that operated within the LCC's boundaries. The rationale of this move was to provide a counterweight to the LCC from below. In time-honoured tradition, the City of London Corporation remained firmly untouched.

Despite the LCC's reputation as an efficient and dedicated authority, by the late 1950s it was widely acknowledged that London had outgrown its nineteenth-century local government institutions. Another Royal Commission was appointed to look at ways of providing a tier of local government that covered the Greater London region rather than just the inner London area that fell under the LCC's jurisdiction. The Commission unanimously recommended the creation of a Greater London Council with as many powers as possible passing to the Boroughs beneath it, these being reduced to 52 in number.

The recommendations were acted upon in the 1963 London Government Act, although the government did amend the size of the proposed authority and created only 32 London Boroughs, with education being passed to the Boroughs other than those that the were originally under the jurisdiction of the LCC (here education was to be supervised by the new Inner London Education Authority). The new system was in fact copied to some extent by the 1972 Local Government Act (which provided a comprehensive two-tier system along similar lines for England and Wales).

The election of Margaret Thatcher's Conservative government in 1979 was shortly followed by Labour's retaking the GLC from the Conservatives in 1981. The two events were significant as they signalled a collision course between the two tiers of government on ideological lines. Tensions over transport policy and the Tory-baiting antics of the GLC's Leader Ken Livingstone saw the demand for abolition intensify (the Tory Boroughs had originally argued for it in the early 1980s) and with the 1985 Local Government Act Londoners found themselves in the same situation as they would have been a century earlier, with the GLC's functions passing to either the Boroughs or a plethora of government-appointed Quangos.

Alongside there being "no such thing as society, only individuals and families", it appeared to Margaret Thatcher that there was no such thing as London, only 32 Boroughs and the City. Until the creation of the Greater London Authority (a directly elected Mayor and 25-member Assembly) in 2000 by the Labour government elected in 1997, London had 14 years in the wilderness without any kind of elected representative tier of government. In addition, under the new system, the extended 'GLA family' means that bodies such as the Metropolitan Police Authority (whose function were previously carried out single-handedly by the Home Secretary) and the new London Fire and Emergency Planning Authority have benefit of being chaired by elected representatives of the people of London. However, governance arrangements in London remain incoherent, even post-GLA. There are 32 London Boroughs that are too small to make any kind of strategic impact, yet too remote to reflect community identity. The City of London Corporation remains unreformed, so Londoners are without any kind of accountable or democratic government in the heart of the capital.

The issues facing Outer London, where Harrow has more in common with Watford in Hertfordshire in terms of transport and education than Lambeth in Inner London, mean that London's political institutions are based on 1965 boundaries designed to electorally favour one political party. To many, these concerns may appear esoteric or divorced from the issues facing voters in the capital, yet taken in the round they affect the ability to deliver services or make an impact in key areas such as economic development.

Scotland

Like many other facets of its political system, the evolution of local government in Scotland has always been closely pegged to that of England. Local administrative units, known as burghs, came into existence during the middle ages for the primary purpose of sustaining trade in local communities and also protecting royal revenues and influence. They eventually assumed more powers to regulate other areas of local life. Like the English parish vestries, the Scottish Church established 'Kirk Sessions' to provide poor relief and basic education on a parochial basis. These activities were financed by both church collections and the rates system, the rate being set on a County basis by 'Commissioners of Supply'. Being similar to the English quarter sessions, they eventually accumulated powers to manage highways and organise local police forces.

By the early nineteenth century however (a century after the Act of Union with England), these unelected units had succumbed to corruption and a lack of competence to deal with the social issues of the day entailed with urban growth. Many burghs were reformed under the 1833 Burghs Reform Acts, although some of the smaller burghs remained untouched until 1900. The middle part of the nineteenth century saw some reform, with the introduction of local elected poor relief boards in 1845, local boards for the care of the mentally ill in 1857 and elected school boards in 1872. Elected County Councils were (as in England) introduced in 1889 and in 1900 the Town Councils (Scotland) Act ensured that all burghs were elected bodies.

In 1918, the school boards were replaced with conventional LEAs based on Counties and large burghs and 1929 the local government system was rationalised into County Councils, 'Counties of Cities' (akin to English County Boroughs), large burghs, small burghs and district Councils. In the 1960s, a Royal Commission headed by Lord Wheatley (running alongside the Redcliffe-Maud Commission) was appointed by the Labour government of Harold Wilson to find ways of reforming the system further. The Commission recommended the reform of Scottish local government along the lines of a largely two-tier system of nine regional Councils and 53 district Councils, with three unitary island Councils and a tier of community Councils at the parish level (where required). The Conservative government at Westminster accepted the Commission's proposals and from 1975 this was the system of local government that operated in Scotland.

As in Wales, the mid 1990s round of local government reorganisation initiated under John Major's Conservative government left Scotland with a wholly unitary system of local government from 1996 onwards, axing the regional Councils in favour of district Councils with altered boundaries. Scottish local government has, since 1999, functioned under the control of the devolved Scottish Parliament.

Wales

In spite of its separate history as a nation, because of Wales' long-standing historic constitutional symmetry with England, Welsh local government owes its genesis to the same circumstances as England and its reform has generally been carried out alongside that of England (Redcliffe-Maud for instance). There are several recent differences between Wales and England however. Welsh elected parochial units are known as Community Councils and following the local government reorganisation of the mid 1990s, Wales was left with a wholly unitary system of local government, ending the two tiers of Counties and districts that had been in place since 1974. The Welsh Assembly has no formal legislative powers over local government in Wales but supervises it in the same way that the Secretary of State for Wales did until the Assembly became live in 1999.

Northern Ireland

Due to the size of the province and the irregular constitutional nature of Northern Ireland as part of the United Kingdom, the role and function of local government differs from the rest of the country. Following the Macrory review of 1970, local government was reorganised into 26 District Councils (elected using proportional representation) and nine Area Boards (a mixture of local Councillors appointed by the districts and ministerial appointees) in 1973. The result of the 1973 reorganisation was the transfer of local services to central government in the province. The traditional six Counties of Northern Ireland (part of the nine Counties of Ulster on the island of Ireland) are now ceremonial only. The residual functions of the District Councils include leisure and environmental services, the licensing of markets and entertainments and food hygiene and trading standards. There are four Area Boards for health and social services and five for education and libraries. There is a single Housing Executive and a Fire Authority for the province.

Other services and the general supervision of local government matters in the province are now administered by the Northern Ireland Assembly ('Stormont').

3 Bread and butter issues

> *'Local government' may have a wide variety of meanings. Since it is 'government,' the system of local government, which a country adopts, must be part of its governmental or constitutional structure. Since it is 'local', it relates to specific portions of the country defined by locality.*[27]
>
> Sir Ivor Jennings

The existence of local government is underpinned by a series of Acts of Parliament, some of which even stem back to the Middle Ages. This legal framework, exercised through statutes and common law, is effectively the constitution of local government and this is based on the premise that local authorities can only perform the functions that Parliament delegates (as opposed to being able to do anything that isn't prohibited by Parliament, as is the norm in other European countries). This issue will be of relevance later with the discussion of demands for a 'Power of General Competence for Local Government'. However, the notion of statutes and common law (decisions taken by the courts that affect local government – e.g. 'Fare's Fair' during the Livingstone era of the GLC) as the Constitution of Local Government should not be confused with the new individual Council constitutions brought in under the Local Government Act 2000, itself a landmark Act in terms of the Constitution.

This situation is a consequence of the lack of a written British constitution as it would be far simpler to state that local authorities are free to do anything Parliament doesn't prohibit them from undertaking under this arrangement. Under our constitutional arrangements, the delivery of local authority services is comprehensively covered by national law and it is from this legislation that local government flows. Furthermore, the delivery of those same services and the wider powers exercised by a local authority are tightly bound by the doctrine of ultra vires. This is the specific legal provision, introduced in the nineteenth century to assuage critics of the extension of democracy (and more recently the anti-socialists of the New Right), that prevents local authorities from acting outside the powers delegated to them by Parliament, and this has in itself led to a number of interesting cases. The legal sanction placed upon local Councillors as the accountable figures in the dealings of any local authority was the power of surcharge (to be held individually liable) and even dismissal from office. The delivery of services is a primary aspect of local government's raison d'etre, alongside its representative and quasi-judicial roles (planning and licensing) of course, although the nuances in debate exist over to what extent should local government be responsible for the delivery of those services, as we will see.

Local government is a complex, diverse and sprawling beast, employing over 2.1m staff and is democratically accountable through over 21 000 elected Councillors serving on our district, County and unitary authorities. Its activities cost £70 billion a year to fund, which accounts for around a quarter of all public spending, although only a quarter of this is generated from collection of the Council Tax. It is a bread and butter concern of politicians but, philosophically speaking, it is an important aspect of self-government at the local level, expressing a degree of autonomy from the central state through a pluralistic set of arrangements validated by regular elections.

Throughout the late nineteenth and the twentieth century, as we have seen, it has played a key role in the evolution of the 'womb-to-tomb' Beveridge welfare state and many of the most controversial issues in terms of social policy have been as a result of local government's actions – the Cleveland child sex abuse scandals, racism and riots in the North, the Victoria Climbie case, to name but a few. Its actions have a great bearing on all of our lives; it is, in essence, the fabric of our democratic well-being and the hallmark of a civilised society. As directly elected bodies, local authorities are unique as features of the sub-national state insofar as they do not merely administer one function (as opposed to the local health authority), they are multi-faceted and provide a diverse range of services. They are defined by the relationship between elected members and Council officers pretty much in the same way that national government is defined by the role of Civil Servants in the implementation of policy and the role of MPs in formulating and being accountable for it.

The enduring values of local democracy have a noble heritage, hailing back to the Greek City-states and Anglo-Saxon folkmoots, and form the basis of the representative self-government of local communities. Through this we derive the purpose of local politics, to administer the local state according to a set of political principles and common goals, although it is not unknown for Independent (that is without a party ticket) candidates to win elections or even control local authorities. The significance of this will be covered in the next chapter. As we have also seen, local government's evolution has mirrored that of urban Britain, with different types of local authority existing to serve different kinds of community, both urban and rural, or in some cases both. This has a bearing on the way services are delivered and the responsibilities held by the different kinds of local authority, as does the presence of other sub-national agencies.

Often referred as a 'political system in miniature', the local state is a distinguished element of our political system and furthermore displays traits that are to be found in other areas of it. In the nineteenth century, Liberal opinion viewed the local state as being of prime importance, with John Stuart Mill articulating that view that local government embodied the liberal democratic principles of 'freedom, participation and efficiency'.[28] For instance, through the values of pluralism brought about by its existence, local government can act as a check against the central state. Furthermore, through the emphasis on participation, through elections (both from voters and candidates) it can 'enrich social life by engendering a spirit of community'.[29] Finally, through its 'territorial diversity', local government can fit in with a set of arrangements that facilitate co-ordinated services rather than the chaos of either laissez-faire or central government ignorance of local circumstances.

The more modern social democratic use of local democracy sees the local state as an important agency in the welfare state, although this presumes a strong role for the centre as well, eroding the Liberal values of participation in the name of redistributing wealth. However, even more recently we have seen this eroded even further under the New Right's attack on the 'nanny state'. These kinds of philosophical boundaries (which are often blurred) are only one part of the story however, with competing claims being mounted for the legitimacy of local government.

The Case for Local Democracy – why the low turnout?

Local government has no independent right to exist. Its continued existence is based on the contribution it can make to good government. It needs to demonstrate that it is a more effective means of government than local administration.[30]

This section will cover two aspects – the specific case for the existence and continuation of local government and the factors that detract from this and have lead to diminishing turnouts in Council elections. As we have seen, local government has come under threat on a number of occasions. Therefore, it is vital to assert the case for local democracy and appreciate why threats have not led to outright abolition or the more considerable diminution of local government's powers beyond what exists today. All too often, local government is seen as a problem to its central government paymaster and guardian. Local government often circumvents the wishes of central government and adds to its financial burden immensely. It should be only too apparent why central government can often lose its patience with local government (some more than others) and why Harold Laski's argument in Chapter One, that "the results of problems not central in their incidence require decision at the place, and by the persons, where and by whom the incidence is most deeply felt"[31] may cease to hold any relevance against these pressures.

Some would argue[32] that this tension displays the vigour and strength of our democracy as a whole as these tensions are more often than not resolved and local government is seen to assert itself against what can often be an over mighty central executive. What instantly comes into play is the top-down nature of this, powers delegated by Parliament, as opposed to the bottom-up versions of local government found in countries such as France, and this is a reoccurring theme in any deliberation on the role of local democracy. The case for local democracy needs to be asserted as it is not protected in this way: central government has proven itself to be quite adept in removing features of it does not care for (the GLC, the Metropolitan Counties, Cleveland County Council), despite the erstwhile role of (unelected) local Councils as the electoral college for Parliament in days of yesteryear. In addition to this, circumstances need to be right for the continuing health of that local democracy, although change in itself can enhance that rather than detract from it, as has been argued.

Local Councils enhance the local identities of the areas they serve in most cases (although perhaps not in the case of Hambleton District Council in North Yorkshire for instance, which serves the towns of Thirsk and Northallerton yet is named after local hills few have actually heard of). Their existence therefore goes beyond concepts of representative democracy and accountability in service provision: only the sternest Fabian planner would advocate local self-government on the basis of districts carved out of proportionate populations regardless of identity or characteristics such as its rural or urban nature.

However, regardless or size or shape, our local authorities possess the same powers and responsibilities delegated to them by a sovereign Parliament which may decide to increase or reduce them at a later date. In addition to reflecting and fostering the concept of local identity, through self-government local Councils promote and facilitate local citizenship and participation in the democratic process. Because of frequency of Council elections, voters are given the opportunity to participate in them more regularly than Parliamentary elections. Conversely, while we are said to have an above average number of legislators at Westminster (when contrasted against a comparable democracy), we also have a lower than average number of local Councils. This notwithstanding, that number could be decreased further under any future reorganisation of local government in England.

This does not, however, take into account the large number of town and parish Councillors (90 000). From 1835 onwards, the role of these diminished as the two-tier system evolved to what it has become today and as a result they are more concerned with small-scale representation than service provision by virtue of their limited powers and role. They are derided by some as irrelevant and hangovers from another era but as we progress to a more unitary system of local government, they could in fact become more relevant and necessary, especially as the notion of local pluralism would be denied without the presence of County and District Councils.

Pluralism is a key factor in demonstrating the need for the continuation of a healthy local democracy. Lord Acton famously stated in a letter to Bishop Mandell Creighton that "power tends to corrupt, and absolute power corrupts absolutely", and any mechanism that can serve as a bulwark against the centralisation of power will hopefully go some way towards preventing this. It would seem that the most appropriate (if not the only) level to fulfil this task would be authority exercised at the sub-national level, i.e. local government. The role of local government as an element of pluralism in our democracy has been recognised by many, including the Widdicombe review (ironically regarded by many in local government as one of the most sustained attacks on local democracy by central government) which stated that "the case for pluralism is that power should not be concentrated in one organisation of state, but should be dispersed, thereby providing political checks and balances, and a restraint on arbitrary government and absolutism."[33]

Therefore it would appear that to deny local self-government or to argue that there is no case for local democracy would be to create more problems than is worth it, regardless of any temptations based on short-term expediency or political fads. There is nothing new in this realisation; classic English empirical philosophy from Thomas Hobbes to Jeremy Bentham recognises nothing less than this. The critique of the local state usually originates from the New Right (although it was Labour's Tony Crosland who proclaimed that "the party's over") flowing from their disdain for the welfare state as a means of encouraging dependency and inefficiency.

Certainly, by centrally-imposed mechanisms such as outsourcing local authority services, the cost of local government could be reduced to an acceptable minimum but the further extension of this was ideological – the New Right harked back to a nineteenth century vision of society prior to the expansion of the welfare state, neglecting to remember that it was local government that began the process of tackling the social and environmental ills so commonly associated with that era. Local government, like the BBC, trade unions and the Church of England, was regarded as one of the barriers to the implementation of Thatcher's agenda. The reforms introduced by that government had the effect of limiting local government's role in a number of key areas, although it is improbable that they could have realistically extended the cull of local authorities beyond the GLC and the Mets.

Even with the most rigorous of assertions and testimonies to its benefits, nothing, but nothing, it seems will convince the public to take voting in local government elections seriously. The struggle for a universal franchise in local government elections was won 20 years later than the struggle for full women's suffrage in Parliamentary elections – only ratepayers (usually the male breadwinner of the household) had the right to participate in local government elections until the reform of 1948. However, the recent decline in the number of people voting in Parliamentary elections (59% in 2001) was pre-dated by trends in local government elections by three decades or so.

Noting the surges in the local elections turnout incurred when they are held alongside a General Election may suggest the oft-cited condition of voter fatigue but this on its own is not a satis-factory excuse for such poor rates of participation in local self-government. Furthermore, the exercise to find candidates to fight local elections is not as fiercely contested within political parties as those involved in selecting Parliamentary candidates, and while the reasons for this may be obvious it is often the case that many party selection contests are occupied by 'any comers' and that a significant number of Council seats go uncontested with winners declared before the campaign even starts. The turnout rates become even more disappointing when one realises that participation is almost a predominantly middle-class affair, with turnouts on Council estates where the need for advocacy and representation is its strongest being pitifully low compared to middle class suburban areas where it is alleged that the electorate is better informed and more likely to complain about issues of local democracy.

A kinder explanation rests on the fact that the dominance of Westminster politics means that local government politics are given less priority by both political parties and the media and this conspires to keep them out of public political discourse and consciousness, with more emphasis being placed on the power of votes for Parliament being able to change anything or send a signal to politicians. This is exacerbated further when one realises that many voters use the local elections to send a signal to politicians at Westminster and while local issues play a part in some election contests (single issue parties or popular local Councillors attracting votes from supporters of other parties) for the most part voting behaviour generally corresponds to feelings generated by issues of national importance.

Another reason articulated (usually by Councillors themselves) is that low turnouts reflect a perception of the reduced importance of local government as a result of the reduction in its powers by central government, although this does not take into account the fact that low turnouts began before this process took root.

Electoral turnout in local government since 1974

Year	London	English Met	English Counties	English Distr (A)	English Distr (P)	Welsh Counties	Welsh Districts	Scottish Regions	Scottish Districts	English Unitaries
74	36.4							50.6	51.4	
75		32.7								
76		38.1		44.7	44.4					
77			42.3					44.7		
78	43.1	37.2			42.4				47.8	
79		74.7		72.1	73.5		76.9			
80		36.3			38.9				45.7	
81			43.7			48.6				
82	43.9	38.8			41.8			42.9		
83		42.0		45.0	45.6		46.3			
84		39.8			40.2				44.4	
85			41.6			45.2				
86	45.4	39.9			41.9			45.6		
87		44.7		48.8	50.6		51.4			
88		40.1			41.5				45.5	
89			39.2			44.2				
90	48.1	46.2			48.6			45.9		
91		40.8		48.2	46.2		53.4			
92		32.5			37.8				41.4	
93			37.2			38.8				
94	46.0	38.9			42.6			45.1		
95		33.8		41.9	39.2		48.8		44.9	39.7
96		30.5			37.2					34.6
97			73.2*							69.7*
98	34.6	24.8			30.8					27.8
99		26.1		35.8	32.5		49.7		59.4	31.5

(A) Elections to whole Council using all seats

(P) Elections to part of Council on electoral cycle basis

* Alongside General Election of same day (1 May 1997)

Apathy was recognised as a symptom of malaise in local democracy some time before it announced its arrival nationally but it is just one aspect of a wider political problem in the disaffection of the governed with their governors.[34] The situation looks even worse when one considers not only the low numbers of black and ethnic minority Councillors in our Council Chambers but also the low participation rates in local elections amongst those communities, although these two problems are far from exclusive from one another.

The problem has been recognised by all concerned (political parties, civil servants and Council officers) although there is disagreement to the extent to which practices must change in order to address it, with modernisation of voting methods (Internet and mobile phone voting) being presented as a panacea for this (for a more detailed argument see www.electoralcommission.gov.uk). So it would seem that even apathy in local government is a 'political football' with 'dividing lines' these days. At the May 2002 local elections, voting behaviour and turnout was keenly observed, mainly by pundits, critics and policy-makers rather than voters themselves, with all eyes falling on the North of England to see if the extremist British National Party could capitalise on recent surges in support following the riots among Asian communities the year before.

Despite intense campaigning across their carefully cultivated pockets of electoral support, the BNP 'breakthrough' was limited to three seats on Burnley Council fortunately (although they subsequently increased their numbers in two Council by-elections in the North of England). Turnout in the elections hovered at around 34% across England as a whole, with the variance being confined to low turnouts in inner City areas and higher turnouts in the Shires, as predicted. One of the more interesting facets of the elections were the electoral 'pilots' used to evaluate if changing aspects of the way people vote (longer hours, electronic counting, voting on the net etc.) led to any increase in turnout. The schemes were generally held to be a success, leading to increased participation and faster counting where used, although some have rushed to advocate their introduction as an overall panacea for deep-rooted problems in local government that manifest themselves in low turnouts.

Electronic/internet voting pilots - May 2002

Local Authority	Type	Turnout % (1998)	Turnout % (2002)
Bolton	Kiosk	25.4	32.7
Chester	Touch-screen	32.3	35.5
Crewe & Nantwich	Website	18.0	31.4
Liverpool	Telephone, internet, text, digital TV	22.1	27.5
Newham (Council)	Smart cards	28.4	26.9
Newham (Mayoral)	Smart cards	N/A	27.6
St Albans	Kiosk, internet	35.5	38.2
Sheffield	Kiosk, internet, text	25.0	30.0
Stratford-upon-Avon	Kiosk	35.0	40.6
Swindon	Internet, touchtone phone (early voting)	25.4	31.2

All areas outside of London using all-postal ballots saw turnout increase; in Chorley it almost doubled from 31.3% to 62.5%. However, there appears to be a psychological impediment towards rolling these pilots out across all British elections, both on the part of conservative Civil Servants and the politicians and activists that make up our political parties.

Reasons for this range from concerns about electoral fraud, to allegations that such methods have been devised in order to minimise the role of political activists. But the figures speak for themselves.

Postal voting Councils – May 2002

Local authority	Turnout % (1998)	Turnout % (2002)
Basingstoke and Deane	28.9	34.3
Chorley	31.3	61.5
Crawley	19.0	34.3
Gateshead	29.3	57.3
Greenwich	32.5	31.9
Hackney	34.8	31.5
Havering	34.3	45.0
Middlesbrough (Mayoral)	N/A	41.0
North Tyneside (Mayoral)	N/A	42.5
North Tyneside (Council)	27.8	42.4
North West Leicestershire	N/A	34.0
Preston	29.0	34.0
South Tyneside	22.4	55.3
Stevenage	25.5	52.9
Trafford	33.7	49.0

The May 2002 local elections were also notable as the first set of elections to be held for directly elected Mayors, although this will be discussed in further detail later. In particular, the voting trend against the main parties can be more acutely observed here in the results of the first set of Mayoralties. It can be argued that voting for a Mayor gives the voter more say in the political control of the Council as a whole, so factors related to individual wards become irrelevant. Furthermore, the candidates seeking election have to base their campaign as much on personality as their political platform.

In Middlesbrough, Ray Mallon won convincingly in a safe Labour stronghold by campaigning on a 'get tough on crime' ticket as well as relying on his own popularity derived from his days as a controversial but popular high profile police chief. The Hartlepool Mayoralty was won by Stuart Drummond, a 20-something call centre employee who also doubled up as 'H'Angus the Monkey' (the mascot for the town's historically unsuccessful football team) on Saturdays, with what began as a joke candidacy thrusting a political unknown into the civic centre in a Borough now characterised by low turnouts and moribund political culture. The second round of Mayoral elections in October 2002 yielded little comfort for Labour (as the party that initiated the introduction of elected Mayors), with Independents snatching victory once again. Such concerns have been amplified in the period following the elections, with those against elected Mayors being able to point at the election of untested mavericks and the future possibility of a BNP Mayor in some areas.

Mayoral elections 2002

Local authority	Previous control (Council)	New control (Mayor)
Bedford	No Overall Control	Independent
Doncaster	Labour	Labour
Hackney	Labour	Labour
Hartlepool	No Overall Control	Independent
Lewisham	Labour	Labour
Mansfield	Labour	Independent
Middlesbrough	Labour	Independent
Newham	Labour	Labour
North Tyneside	Labour	Conservative
Stoke-on-Trent	No Overall Control	Independent
Watford	Labour	Liberal Democrat

Some confusion exists as to the extent to which local government provides local services, with services previously administered by local government (health visiting and further education, for instance) now in the hands of other bodies. As a result of the expansion in the 'Quango state' during the 1980s and 1990s (it is a little known fact that Margaret Thatcher entered office pledging to reduce its size), its functions were considerably curtailed and while local citizens still refer to "the Council" in relation to service issues, they may in fact be mistaken in a number of cases. The Quango state aside for a moment, local government is still responsible for a wide range of services that touch upon every area of our lives and this section will attempt to deal with the 'nuts and bolts' of how this takes place.

However, the role and nature of those services now are considerably different from the situation local government found itself in around the time of the Royal Commission of Inquiry into the Municipal Corporations in the mid-nineteenth century, although earlier chapters have dealt with the political history and context of this. In order to examine this, light must be cast over both the powers and responsibilities of local government as a service provider. This is covered by this section, whereas consideration of the local Council as a representative political organ and the local authority as a corporate body and service provider, is examined in later chapters.

Indeed, local government would be nothing more than a mere 'talking shop' unless it was tied in to provision of important local services (see therefore the criticisms levelled at Parish Councils) and it is nothing but flexible in terms of the responsibilities heaped on (and taken away from) it over the years. These are the dividing lines between the national political parties at Westminster over the issue of local government and we have seen the extent to which local government has a multitude of functional portfolios (housing, education, environment) that tie in closely to national priorities, hence its position as a battleground over the welfare state in the 1980s. Thus local government suffered, not the political parties that used it as a battering ram against each other.

This is far from an esoteric debate as it gets to the heart of Parliament's role as the body responsible for the conferral of powers and duties to local government under the principles of both Parliamentary sovereignty and ultra vires. The duties conferred by Parliament are either compulsory or optional, depending on the nature of the service to be provided. The only way a local authority can achieve extra powers outside of the current law is to promote a specific Private Bill in Parliament, which was common in the nineteenth century (see Chapter Two) but not as common today due to the costs involved, although the 33 local Councils in London often promote a London Local Authorities Bill for this purpose. But it is from this legislation that a local authority's power to deliver services is derived, leaving a complex legal minefield in place. Furthermore, the political 'dividing lines' (within parties as well as between them) have long been concerned with the extent to which local authorities either deliver services directly or just attempt to plan and regulate them.

The type of local authority (district or County) determines the services it delivers, except in the case of the unitary authority (see Appendix IV). However, the extent to which it delivers or regulates them is conditional upon the principles of Best Value and how they are applied in that authority (see Chapter Seven). The range of services provided places some local authorities alongside multi-national corporations in terms of the staff they employ and the revenues they generate from their activities – Kent County Council outstrips both Beechams and Burmah Oil in this regard. Generally speaking, local government remains responsible for the following key services according to the powers delegated to it by Parliament:

Powers delegated to local authorities

	Joint Authorities	Met Councils	London Boroughs^	District Councils	Unitary Authorities	County Councils
Education		•	•		•	•
Housing		•	•	•	•	
Planning Applications		•	•	•	•	
Strategic Planning		•	•		•	•
Passenger Transport	•				•	•
Highways		•	•		•	•
Fire	•				•	
Social Services		•	•		•	•
Libraries		•	•		•	•
Leisure and Recreation		•	•	•	•	
Waste Collections		•	•	•	•	
Waste Disposal	•	•	•		•	•
Environmental Health		•	•	•	•	
Revenue Collection		•	•	•	•	

* Joint Fire authorities operate in Counties with unitary authorities in them.

^ A number of functions are now carried out by the Greater London Authority such as; passenger transport (through Transport for London), economic development (through the London Development Agency) and Fire (through the London Fire and Emergency Planning Authority).

However, as previously stated, which authority carries these out in any local area is governed by the types (or type, in the case of unitaries) of authority serving that area.

Education is the largest local authority function, although under the reforms of the 1980s and 1990s it has shrunk in size through the loss of its Higher Education (Polytechnics) and Further Education (Tertiary Colleges and Sixth Forms). During this time there was, on average, an Education Act every year that introduced new aspects of management into the state schools system such as the Local Management of Schools (LMS), which transferred considerable budgetary powers for individual schools from local authorities as LEAs to each school governing body.

The 1988 Education Act also introduced a National Curriculum and the testing of pupils at age 7, 11 and 14 as part of attainment targets. A notable education reform under New Labour has been the extension of OFSTED's inspection regime to LEAs (as opposed to just individual schools) and the creation of Learning and Skills Councils. Education is administered by LEAs at the County level where the two tier remains or Metropolitan and Unitary authorities in all other areas. Social Services are another important local authority service, particularly in the context of the post-war welfare state, although items such as the payment of social benefits are administered by central government.

The foundations for modern local authority social services were laid by the National Assistance Act of 1948 and Social Services are often among the most controversial of local government's activities, dealing with residential and domiciliary care for the elderly, child protection, counselling and fostering and adoption. It is provided at the same tier as Education (Counties, Mets and Unitaries). Similarly local authority Housing (carried out at District or Metropolitan District level) played a major part in the post-war welfare state, although this was halted by both the 'right to buy' introduced by the Tories in 1980, and the freeze on the use of local authority Housing Revenue Accounts for the purposes of house-building (although local authorities were permitted to access £5bn of their capital receipts for this purpose once Labour was back in power at Westminster) and the Local Government and Housing Act of 1989 prohibited, inter alia, local authority rent subsidies.

Planning responsibilities are governed by a series of Town and Country Planning Acts and are shared between the various tiers, with Counties (or equivalent) exercising a strategic planning role through Structure Plans, whereas the Districts exercise powers over development control by approving or rejecting applications made by businesses and the public (from retail parks to an extension on a house). A recent development is the proposal to reform the Planning system by removing the Structure Plans at County level and Unitary Development Plans and replacing them with regional spatial plans.

Like Planning, Licensing and Market Trading is a quasi-judicial function performed by Councillors sat in committee and using their judgement on individual applications and appeals according to criteria laid down by Parliament. This role is concerned with alcohol and entertainments licences and the regulation of local markets, being carried out at District level (or equivalent).

The local authority Passenger Transport and Highways function varies according to where the Council is situated, with Passenger Transport Executives (and Transport for London in the capital) in Metropolitan areas overseeing the operation of public transport whereas in other areas the role is limited to minor regulation following the deregulation of buses and the sell-offs of many local authority bus companies (Cleveland Transit and Newcastle Busways for instance). However, all roads (except major trunk roads) are maintained by local authorities, who are also responsible for all aspects of road safety and traffic management.

Police and Fire Authorities are now independent of local authorities, albeit with statutory local authority representation on them. As a 'discretionary' function, Leisure and Recreation is often the barometer for the financial health of the tier that administrates it whereas Libraries are considered to be an integral element of local authority education, culture and communications and are hugely popular with those who use them, being as there are no alternative providers.

Waste Management is also split between the Counties and Districts, with Districts collecting refuse and Counties taking care of its disposal (or both in the case of Mets and Unitaries), whereas the Environmental Health function is concerned with pollution control, inspection of unfit dwellings and premises for food preparation and consumption – basically the functions associated with local authorities over a century ago. This is also concerned with some of the more salacious and 'interesting' activities that local authorities can concern themselves with such as the licensing of local sex shops or their duties under the Zoo Act to keep tranquilliser guns in case of escaped wild animals.

Councils' role in Economic Development involves working with local businesses to promote job creation and regeneration and is carried out at all tiers, although bodies such as the Urban Development Corporations (1980-1998) and Training and Enterprise Councils took over major aspects of this role. Finally, Revenue Collection is the responsibility of District Councils (or equivalent) to collect the Council Tax (the 'Uniform Business Rate' is collected locally but distributed by central government grant – see the section on Finance) and arrange the payment of precept any other tiers (Parish and Town Councils or County Councils/GLA).

Local government finance for dummies

If the world of local government per se seems mundane, then the world of local government finance, with its Chartered Institute of Public Finance and Accountancy, Area Cost Adjustments and Revenue Support Grants, can seem possibly deathly boring – local government bores, but local government finance bores absolutely (to paraphrase Lord Acton). Hence the brevity of this section. Local government finance is regarded as one of the most important issues of local government by central government; the recent welter of

White Papers and legislation issued is concerned with the financial regimes of local authorities, with a few mentions of democratic engagement thrown in for good measure. Local government treats it with earnest seriousness too – it has huge consequences for Councillors and Council officers alike, it is the numero uno bread and butter issue of them all.

The issue has received more than its first share of central government attention and represents one of the more interesting dynamics between the centre and the local state, hence Crosland's statement that "The party's over". However, central government had already begun to grapple with this issue with the Layfield Committee on Local Government Finance, through the activities of Mrs Thatcher in the 1980s and ending with the financial regime of New Labour. It has seen 25 years of prolific activity and constant change, culminating in the recent White Paper (which will be covered later). The section will deal with the basics and give a political context to central government attempts to grapple with the thorny issue that is local government finance.

Local government finance is significant for the same reason that finance is significant in any area of the public sector – it has a direct bearing on our lives. The pressure to do more with less is as acute in local government as in any other area of the public sector. Financial circumstances vary according to type and location of local authority and the pressures they face – North Tyneside will have different budgetary pressures compared to North Somerset. Finance has proved itself to be one of the more controversial areas of local government activity – the riots in Trafalgar Square in 1990 were fundamentally concerned with local government finance in the form of the much-maligned Poll Tax or Community Charge.[35] It has been the scene of revolt in local government, with challenges being mounted by renegade local Councils to central government's capping regime. But for most people it will be hard to see what all the fuss is about, unless a particularly excessive Council Tax Bill lands on their doorstep or their child's school is closed down.

Each year a local Council must meet to set the Budget for the local authority's spending over the forthcoming year. This enables the Council to set the priority areas for Council spending on local services. Most British citizens over a certain age are aware of this and could follow this. However, most would turn away from any discussion beyond this basic state of affairs. The Council's Budget is concerned with two areas of spending – Revenue Expenditure and Capital Expenditure. Revenue Expenditure is concerned with bread and butter concerns such as wages and salaries, fuel for the Council's fleet of vehicles, office equipment, catering in elderly persons' homes, schoolbooks etc., whereas Capital Expenditure is concerned with major items that will bring long-term benefits for the local community such as school buildings, new roads, leisure centres etc.

However, Councils are tightly bound by rules set by the government in terms of what they can spend and on what – for instance Councils' ability to borrow money to fund their activities is strictly controlled to the point whereby it is hard to even contemplate doing so. It is possible for local authorities to instigate creative accounting methods to get round this however.[36] In the first instance, a local Council is informed of its Basic Credit Approval by central government. This imposes a ceiling upon how much a local authority can borrow to fund capital projects and sometimes a Supplementary Credit Approval is granted to fund government priority areas for local spending. In addition, a Council may sell some of its assets to generate capital receipts (such as housing or land) to fund its spending activities, although again this is controlled by government-imposed ceilings.

Service Inspections in key areas of provision such as education and social services, as well as the way the local authority uses the resources available to it, form the third stage of the assessment using performance indicators to gauge how well the Council is and should be performing. Finally, all aspects of financial management count towards the final score in terms of stewardship of resources and providing value for money to local citizens. The inspection regime in local government has grown to an unprecedented level over the last 20 years – it is hoped that the CPA process will simplify, stream-line and reduce the burden of inspections on Councils.

The end result of CPA is that each local authority is presented with a 'balanced scorecard' that places each Council into a 'league' alongside other Councils. The 2001 Local Government White Paper proposed four categories, identifying each local authority as either High-performing, Striving, Coasting or Poor-performing. Since then, the Audit Commission has changed the categories to Excellent, Good, Fair, Weak and Poor. At the end of this process, following any grading, local authorities are then exempted from some aspects of regulation, are subjected to agreed targets for improvement or face direct inter-vention in the delivery of services. A different approach to District Councils will take place, with performance assessed on 'cross-cutting' inspections on themes such as 'balanced housing markets' and 'clean, green and safe public space', in addition to performance indicators and self-assessment.

By the end of 2004, the Audit Commission will have carried out a CPA in every local authority in England, something akin towards being the equivalent of an OFSTED Report (the five-yearly appraisal of a school's performance) for local authorities. The banding of local Councils into league tables according to category was a contentious process – with the media latching on to the 'Poor' local authorities 'named and shamed' in the process. Furthermore, this provoked a backlash from both local Councils (especially those in the bottom two categories) and the Local Government Information Unit (a local authority and trade union-funded 'think tank'), who remarked that CPA was nothing more than the opinions of an unelected and unaccountable Quango. However, it is more than likely that the government will continue to use the CPA process in its drive to raise standards in local public services.

4   Mavericks and technocrats – the personnel of local government

This chapter will attempt to deal with, as it states, the personnel of local government. It is not limited to 'personnel' in terms of Council staff as local government would not be government (it would in fact be local administration) without the 21,000 or so local Councillors that make it a political concern. In some respects it would be simplistic to argue that the relationship between Council officers and elected members replicates that of MPs at Westminster and Civil Servants of Whitehall, but it does. However, the Tufton-Buftons and Sir Humphreys of SW1 in the past were more likely to find their opposite numbers in local government to be the dutiful Town Clerks of yesteryear, who similarly were invited to Buckingham Palace to attend an annual garden party with the great and the good during their careers and then to receive a gong of some kind at the end of it.

Like Civil Servants they are meant to be apolitical and provide a degree of permanency, compared to the 'here today, gone tomorrow' politicians of differing administrations. Councillors, unlike MPs however, are elected for fixed terms and usually sit in constituencies with other elected members, as opposed to the single seat nature of an MP's constituency. Furthermore, in most cases, being a Councillor is not a full-time job, unlike an MP and it certainly doesn't carry the same prestige as being an MP. To this end it is worth dividing elected members and officers into separate examinations at this point.

Councillors, elections and the Law

Getting elected as a Councillor is hard enough insofar as you need to get selected by a political party for a ward in which you have a reasonable chance of being chosen by the electorate to represent them as their elected representative in the Town (or County) Hall. Later in this section we will discuss the particular circumstances involved in this process. But being eligible to stand for election in the first place incurs its own set of hurdles. Firstly, a person must be 21 or over to stand for any public office (MP, Councillor, member of devolved body etc) in Britain, even though they can vote from 18 onwards. This is because when the legislation was passed to lower the voting age from 21 to 18 in 1969, MPs felt that 18 year olds should not seek to stand for Parliament or the Council, whereas it now seems like an anachronism more than anything else. The main criteria are inclusion on the electoral register or working in the local authority area for at least 12 months prior to the elections. Furthermore, Council employees (regardless of grade) are automatically debarred from standing for election in the authority in which they work, for obvious reasons.

All local government officers of PO4 grade and above are also prevented for standing in elections to any local authority under the Local Government and Housing Act 1989. Also prevented from standing for election to their local Council are undischarged bankrupts, those convicted of corrupt or illegal electoral practices

Local Councils at District and Unitary level are referred to as Billing Authorities as they have the responsibility for revenue collection and a portion of this (the 'precept') may have to be passed on to Parish or County Councils and Police and Fire Authorities. However, the Council Tax they collect is only a minor proportion of the income they receive, with specific service charges (use of leisure centres, school meals, cost of burials etc) and government grant topping up the total required. Government grants are of particular significance here. The block grant provided to local authorities from central government is known as the Revenue Support Grant (RSG). This is the individual payment made to a local authority from the government's Total Standard Spending, whereby it decides how much of its budget it deems appropriate for local government.

The process of determining how much RSG an individual local authority should receive was until very recently known as its Standard Spending Assessment (SSA) and this was crucial in terms of balancing the local authority's books – if the government under-estimates the amount required then services will need to be cut back and this can be politically disastrous for the local Council concerned. This has recently been replaced with the Formula Funding Shares (FFS) system, with funding levels being determined by Ministers as a means to encourage redistribution of funds across the country.

However, on top of the Council Tax, RSG and receipts is the Uniform Business Rate. Before this was reformed a local authority received all the business rates collected in that locality. Since the introduction of the Uniform Business Rate in 1990 however, while business rates are collected locally they are then aggregated nationally and then forwarded back to the local authority, to their financial detriment in some cases. Local government finance – it may be boring to many but it's a very contentious issue to some.

The end of producer politics – Compulsory Competitive Tendering

Compulsory Competitive Tendering (CCT) was a hallmark policy in terms of the Thatcherite agenda for local government. Competitive Tendering was already commonplace in Tory local authorities such as the London Borough of Wandsworth by the end of the 1980s, but CCT had the effect of, under national direction, obliging other (mainly Labour) local authorities to put their services out to tender so that private sector firms could bid (alongside local Councils' own in-house service providers) for the contracts to provide them. Again, lines in the sand were drawn in dogma – the Tory central government and local authorities being convinced that the private sector would provide better value for money, whereas the Labour Opposition and local authorities argued strongly that services were best kept in-house and in the public sector.

However, while some services were contracted out to private sector contractors under CCT, most notably refuse collection, school meals and grounds maintenance, in many cases local authority in-house service providers won contracts, albeit under strict monitoring financial arrangements and service delivery targets. This notwithstanding, CCT had the effect of installing a culture change that reached all parts of local government's activities and was one of the defining aspects of the 1979–97 Conservative governments' relationship with local government.

CCT was first introduced for construction, maintenance and highways work by the Local Government, Planning and Land Act 1980. It was extended to other blue-collar services, such as refuse collection and ground maintenance, through the Local Government Act 1988. Sport and leisure management was added as a further defined activity through secondary legislation in 1989, and other blue-collar activities were added in 1994. During 1996, the first phases of CCT for local authority professional services were implemented, involving legal, construction and property and personnel services in London and Metropolitan authorities. The Best Value regime introduced by the Labour government has ostensibly replaced CCT with a less rigid definition of the 'compulsory' aspect of CCT, giving local authorities the ability to be more flexible in the way they decide how services are provided and by whom.

CCT was applied to a wide range of local authority services. A local authority could only carry out certain defined activities in-house, through its own Direct Labour Organisation (DLO) or Direct Services Organisation (DSO), if the work had first gone out to tender and been won in open competition. The process involved a comparison of the costs of in-house provision with those of interested private sector service providers. In 1985, the Transport Act saw local authority bus and airport companies subject to the rigours of the market, with the effect of eventually phasing out the municipal provision of local buses in all but a handful of Councils and ending what had begun in the 'gas and water socialism' era. Ideologically-speaking this was the application of New Right principles to local government, breaking down the monopoly of service provision in the vast public sector, of which local government still constituted a major element.

More specifically to local government, the thinking from the Department of the Environment (which then looked after local government) under Nicholas Ridley's tenure as Environment Secretary at the time, was of local Councils as 'enabling authorities', which under the Tory version of the term meant local authorities as the regulator and funder of services rather than the provider of them. While this term has now gained acceptance across local government it more pragmatically seen as Councils presiding over a mixed economy of service provision rather than either a local state monopoly or one hundred per cent privately provided services.

The new inspection regime – Comprehensive Performance Assessment

A significant milestone in local government's history, the Comprehensive Performance Assessment (CPA) heralds a new era of inspection and performance monitoring of local government by the centre. Central government is already able to concern itself with the affairs of any local authority through the District Auditor, who works in the town hall but reports to and works for the Audit Commission. CPA was introduced as a result of the 2001 Local Government White Paper *Strong Local Leadership – Quality Public Services* which states that with CPA "The aim is to free up Councils to innovate and deliver tangible improvements in the quality of services and effective community leadership."[37]

At the core of this is an inspection regime overseen by the Audit Commission that examines each local authority's corporate working to analyse performance in a number of key areas: the quality of local services, strength of financial management and the proven capacity to deliver service improvements. Assessment takes four forms. Firstly, local Councils are asked to analyse their own performance in terms of its achievements and areas of weakness. A Corporate Assessment Team (including an officer and elected member from other 'peer' local authorities) then looks at the Council's corporate approach to the way it does business, enabling the inspection process to be more critical and objective.

Service Inspections in key areas of provision such as education and social services, as well as the way the local authority uses the resources available to it, form the third stage of the assessment using performance indicators to gauge how well the Council is and should be performing. Finally, all aspects of financial management count towards the final score in terms of stewardship of resources and providing value for money to local citizens. The inspection regime in local government has grown to an unprecedented level over the last 20 years – it is hoped that the CPA process will simplify, stream-line and reduce the burden of inspections on Councils.

The end result of CPA is that each local authority is presented with a 'balanced scorecard' that places each Council into a 'league' alongside other Councils. The 2001 Local Government White Paper proposed four categories, identifying each local authority as either High-performing, Striving, Coasting or Poor-performing. Since then, the Audit Commission has changed the categories to Excellent, Good, Fair, Weak and Poor. At the end of this process, following any grading, local authorities are then exempted from some aspects of regulation, are subjected to agreed targets for improvement or face direct inter-vention in the delivery of services. A different approach to District Councils will take place, with performance assessed on 'cross-cutting' inspections on themes such as 'balanced housing markets' and 'clean, green and safe public space', in addition to performance indicators and self-assessment.

By the end of 2004, the Audit Commission will have carried out a CPA in every local authority in England, something akin towards being the equivalent of an OFSTED Report (the five-yearly appraisal of a school's performance) for local authorities. The banding of local Councils into league tables according to category was a contentious process – with the media latching on to the 'Poor' local authorities 'named and shamed' in the process. Furthermore, this provoked a backlash from both local Councils (especially those in the bottom two categories) and the Local Government Information Unit (a local authority and trade union-funded 'think tank'), who remarked that CPA was nothing more than the opinions of an unelected and unaccountable Quango. However, it is more than likely that the government will continue to use the CPA process in its drive to raise standards in local public services.

4   Mavericks and technocrats – the personnel of local government

This chapter will attempt to deal with, as it states, the personnel of local government. It is not limited to 'personnel' in terms of Council staff as local government would not be government (it would in fact be local administration) without the 21,000 or so local Councillors that make it a political concern. In some respects it would be simplistic to argue that the relationship between Council officers and elected members replicates that of MPs at Westminster and Civil Servants of Whitehall, but it does. However, the Tufton-Buftons and Sir Humphreys of SW1 in the past were more likely to find their opposite numbers in local government to be the dutiful Town Clerks of yesteryear, who similarly were invited to Buckingham Palace to attend an annual garden party with the great and the good during their careers and then to receive a gong of some kind at the end of it.

Like Civil Servants they are meant to be apolitical and provide a degree of permanency, compared to the 'here today, gone tomorrow' politicians of differing administrations. Councillors, unlike MPs however, are elected for fixed terms and usually sit in constituencies with other elected members, as opposed to the single seat nature of an MP's constituency. Furthermore, in most cases, being a Councillor is not a full-time job, unlike an MP and it certainly doesn't carry the same prestige as being an MP. To this end it is worth dividing elected members and officers into separate examinations at this point.

Councillors, elections and the Law

Getting elected as a Councillor is hard enough insofar as you need to get selected by a political party for a ward in which you have a reasonable chance of being chosen by the electorate to represent them as their elected representative in the Town (or County) Hall. Later in this section we will discuss the particular circumstances involved in this process. But being eligible to stand for election in the first place incurs its own set of hurdles. Firstly, a person must be 21 or over to stand for any public office (MP, Councillor, member of devolved body etc) in Britain, even though they can vote from 18 onwards. This is because when the legislation was passed to lower the voting age from 21 to 18 in 1969, MPs felt that 18 year olds should not seek to stand for Parliament or the Council, whereas it now seems like an anachronism more than anything else. The main criteria are inclusion on the electoral register or working in the local authority area for at least 12 months prior to the elections. Furthermore, Council employees (regardless of grade) are automatically debarred from standing for election in the authority in which they work, for obvious reasons.

All local government officers of PO4 grade and above are also prevented for standing in elections to any local authority under the Local Government and Housing Act 1989. Also prevented from standing for election to their local Council are undischarged bankrupts, those convicted of corrupt or illegal electoral practices and those with unspent convictions. However, if someone is eligible to stand and has been selected by a political party to represent them as a candidate in a Council election, they then require a sufficient number of votes (usually more than the opposing candidates!) to get them elected to serve as a Councillor for four years. To be able to vote, an elector must be on the local authority's electoral register, which is an easier task now 'rolling registration' has been introduced. Eligibility for inclusion is limited to being 18 or over, a British or EU citizen and not being convicted of electoral fraud. Elections take place every four years in all local authorities, although the method of holding them varies according to their type:[38]

Type of Authority	Electoral cycle and warding arrangements	2000	2001	2002	2003	2004
County Councils	Full Council elections. Single member electoral divisions		FC			
London Boroughs	Full Council elections. Multimember wards			FC		
Metropolitan Districts	By thirds. All wards have three Members	1/3		1/3	1/3	1/3
88 Shire Districts and 14 Unitaries (2002)	By thirds. Almost all wards have between 1-3 members	1/3		1/3	1/3	1/3
150 Shire Districts and various Unitaries	Full Council elections. Almost all wards have 1-3 members			FC		
Greater London Authority	Full Council elections and Mayor who is directly elected London wide	FC				FC
Welsh Unitaries	Full Council elections. Around half are single member				FC	

It is not only Councilors who have to conform to strict laws concerning their activities. Council officers are tightly governed in terms of what they can and cannot do in their communications functions, especially around election time. The Local Government Acts of 1986 and 1988 and the Code of Conduct on Local Government Publicity, like Section 28, the Widdicombe Ban and the abolition of the GLC, were brought in during a politically-charged period of local government's existence, particularly in the light of local authorities using Council publicity to attack central government policies.

This notwithstanding however, local authorities now employ sophisticated communications strategies – to advertise consultation exercises, access to services, changes in the way a local authority is run etc., and much of this legislation is obsolete, even though it still continues to place strenuous demands upon local authorities in terms of monitoring whether or not they are within the law. Another recent development is the duty to promote the economic, environmental and social well-being of the community under the Local Government Act 2000. The use of Council communications to promote the concept of well-being raises several pertinent issues around the law on Council publicity as it stands.

The Local Government Act 1972 lays down initial guidance on Council publicity such as the need for Council communications to be informative rather than seeking to persuade towards any partic-ular point of view and governs the use of funds for publicity – for instance publicising the closure of Council services over Christmas. In addition, local authorities have the power to conduct local research and publicise the results. The laws also cover the behaviour of Council officers and the promotion of what could be construed as party political views around election time. This also applies in the run-up to any Council referendum, with any publicity being required to be anodyne and merely relating to arrangements for polling etc. Finally, one of the most controversial aspects of local authority communications is the now infamous Section 28 of the Local Government Act 1988. This prevents local authorities from 'promoting' homosexuality in any way and was a knee-jerk reaction to tabloid sensationalism over claims that left-wing LEAs were aggressively promoting 'deviant lifestyles'.

The Labour government's attempts at repeal in the 2000 Parliament failed due to entrenched opposition in the House of Lords and a campaign led by the religious right; in the end the government gave way in order to save other aspects of the Local Government Bill it was promoting at the time (including elected Mayors), although it did lead to the defection of Shaun Woodward MP from the Tories. Section 28 has not led to one single case being brought to court under it and it is claimed that schools are wary of investigating homophobic bullying for fear of falling foul under it. Areas in which local authorities could fall foul under it include discouraging discrimination against lesbians and gays, allowing theatre plays with a homosexual theme to be staged on Council property or supporting local Gay Pride events. However, some local authorities such as Bristol have argued that the Human Rights Act 1998 means that their services should be accessible to all groups, including lesbians and gay men.

An executive/scrutiny split – the changing role of the Councillor

The mode of election for Councillors has not changed since the Victorian age, save for a few modifications of the franchise. Councillors can play a variety of roles on the Council. Firstly, all Councillors represent a constituency/ward seat and act as its representative in the Town Hall, providing their constituents with a link to the workings of the Council. They may be asked to look into a constituent's casework issue with the Council such as their place on the local authority's housing waiting list or be asked to represent community views on a planning application to the relevant committee chair. Most Councillors sit on at least one committee or sub-committee of the Council and represent the Council on outside bodies.

A smaller number are chosen by their fellow Councillors to act as Chairs and Vice Chairs of committees and an 'elite' fulfil leadership roles on the Council such as Deputy Leader, Leader or Mayor. However, detail around the nature of these roles has changed immensely over the past five years, more so than over the past century, affecting the role of political parties and the law also. They are public figures (in theory, surveys reveal that less than one in five can name the leader of their Council) yet the business of their coronation into political figures takes place well away from the public gaze.

The British 'Committee system' of local government came into existence in 1835. It naturally follows that every area of local authority activity cannot be micromanaged by the Council as one committee and the multi-functional nature of local government dictates that separate committees are required to supervise individual service areas or political concerns. Depending on the type of Council and the services it provided, each committee shadowed a service department such as Housing, Education and Leisure, as well as cross-cutting issues such as Equalities, Personnel and Finance.

However, each of these were sub-committees of the whole Council.

The virtues of the committee system were held up by political theorist Harold Laski as being "one of the fundamental English contributions to the difficult art of self-government" and its recent passing away, not surprisingly, has been lamented by some backbench Councillors, who feel that the new arrangements have left them behind. Critics of the system (see Chapter seven) argued that the system had not been reformed since the creation of elected local government itself and that it lacked focus and leadership. The new system brought in under the Local Government Act 2000 introduced three new forms of executive governance – Leader and Cabinet, Directly Elected Mayor and Council Cabinet, and Directly Elected Mayor and Council Manager. The differences are covered in greater detail in Chapter seven but most local authorities have opted for the Leader and Cabinet system.

This deviates from the traditional Committee System as the executive is no longer the Leader, Deputy Leaders and the Committee chairs, but the Leader and his or her Cabinet, with each member having a policy portfolio (Regeneration, Housing, Lifelong Learning etc). Their decisions are then 'scrutinised' by a general overview and scrutiny committee and themed scrutiny committees reflecting the portfolios. But the role of Council remains the same as it formally agrees policy and major decisions over budgetary matters and is still chaired by the Mayor or Council Chair.

Additional modernisation measures have been introduced recently such as allowances for Councillors that reflect the work they do rather than merely the number of committee meetings they attend. It is also hoped that these allowances, that make provision for time off work for Council duties, will attract new people to local government who may have previously ruled out running for Council on financial grounds. The purpose of the reforms is to have a focused executive with a clear political leadership role and to enable backbench Councillors to become 'community champions' by scrutinising the executive and having more time to spend in their community, meeting constituents or attending community groups' meetings, under the new arrangements. For an institution obsessed with the long hours 'meetings culture' old habits will certainly die hard. The other slightly more hidden intention is to make political leadership more attractive for those who would bring talents to the job from the world of business or the voluntary sector but who would not have the inclination to run for office under the old system. However, it has been widely reported that those Councillors not belonging to the Cabinet are far from content with this system.

The representative Council – gender, age and race in the Council Chamber

Local Councils are supposed to be reflective of the communities they serve and while they may have traditionally acted as microcosms of society politically (simplistically expressed as working class Councillors being Labour, middle class Councillors being Tory, although there are many exceptions to this), most local Councils do not reflect wider society in terms of gender, age or race. The notion of Councils being more representative of the community is associated with the drive for better decision-making in local government and some of the moves towards modernisation have been made with this in mind. However, there is clearly some way to go as these statistics suggest:

Percentage of Councillors in England and Wales by gender:[39]

Male	71.3
Female	27.9

Percentage of Councillors in England and Wales by ethnicity:[40]

White	97.4
Ethnic Minority	2.5

Percentage of Councillors in England and Wales by age:[41]

Age	%
Under 25	0.1
25-34	3.2
35-44	10.9
45-54	24.3
55-64	34.5
65-74	22.9
75+	4.1

Statistics such as these merely lead to frustration with local government on the part of many, central government and the electorate included. The deficit of representative Councillors has been recognised by central government and the Cantle report into the race riots in the North of England in 2001 touched upon it as a reason for the lack of responsive community leadership in local authorities.[42] There are several reasons why local authorities have traditionally been unrepresentative of local communities:

1 Time commitment. Younger people and those with full time jobs and/or families often cannot find the time to devote to undertaking the responsibilities associated with being a Councillor.

2 Hyper-activism. Councillors tend be drawn from the ranks of well-established party activists.

3 Selection Disadvantage. Conservatism on the part of those selecting ward candidates means that older, white party members who are (or resemble) existing Councillors are likely to find favour with those selecting them.

4 Familiarity Disadvantage. A sizeable number of existing Councillors are degree-educated and from public sector backgrounds and therefore have familiarity with the system. The lack of such familiarity may be intimidating to other putative Councillors.

5 The 'weirdo' effect. Other than those who the rest of society would consider to be 'odd', who would have the bureaucratic stamina to want to spend their lives in committee meetings?

These factors all, to lesser or greater extents, influence both the decision of people to stand for Council and the behaviour of those selecting them as candidates. Political parties such as the Labour Party have made some effort to try to draw candidates from outside the narrow base of run-of-the-mill party activists and measures such as term limits for Councillors have been mooted as a means to give more people the opportunity to become Councillors.

Not all Councillors and observers are signed up to the idea of a more representative local democracy, with claims that age brings with it experience and service, whereas more young and ethnic minority Councillors would just be pandering to a 'tick box mentality'. However, like other aspects of modernisation such as the end of the committee system and the introduction of Councillors' allowances, the drive for more representative Councils is seen by the 'forces of conservatism' in local government as yet another stick for central government to beat the 'old guard' with. Similarly, the introduction of allowances has made it harder to encourage time-servers to retire.

The local party machine and political administration

Election agents often refer to their candidates as 'the legal necessity' for reasons best kept to themselves. But the selection of candidates is only one part of the story in terms of the relationship that Councillors (with a registered party affiliation) enjoy with local party members. To stand a reasonable chance of being elected as a Councillor on a local authority it is usually preferable to be standing on a party ticket, although it is not unknown for Independents, 'Ratepayers' and local parties (the 'People's

Party' who hold the balance of power in Barrow-in-Furness for instance) to get elected. Indeed in Epsom and Ewell Borough Council, residents' associations hold political control. The indicative strength of the political parties in local government is shown here:

Party representation in English and Welsh local Councils (2001):[43]

Conservative	32.9
Labour	36.3
Liberal Democrat	20.5
Green Party	0.9
Plaid Cymru	0.4
Independent	8.0
Other	1.0

Political parties in local government are significant for a number of reasons. Firstly, the local party machine assists in getting its selected candidates elected using an army of volunteers to campaign for them through canvassing and leafleting. Those candidates that are elected Councillors then assemble as a party group and choose their candidates for the elections on the Council to committee chair and civic posts such as Leader and Mayor at the first Council Annual Meeting.

If a political party has the majority of seats on a Council then as the majority group it has the power to choose its candidates for the positions to be elected to by virtue of its majority status. If it is not able to form an overall majority then it will have to co-operate with one or more other parties on the Council, with positions being allocated on a pro rata basis according to party strength. The majority group is important as this imposes discipline on its members, who having discussed and voted for or against a policy or nomination in the party group meeting must then support and vote for it in full Council or committee, under the whipping system.

To vote against or publicly attack any decision made by the majority group can lead to the group imposing discipline on the member, although this varies from party to party. Political parties of significant strength in local government such as Labour and the Tories have formal arrangements for their party groups such as Group Officers, Whips and Local Government Committees (which consist of local activists) to shadow them and national bodies such as the Association of Labour Councillors, whereas the Liberal Democrats (and to a lesser extent the Greens) have more relaxed structures that reflect their commitment to pluralism and participation (although there is an Association of Liberal Democrat Councillors).

The procedures for selecting Labour candidates are very formalised, with minimum membership requirements, vetting by the Local Government Committee and often gruelling selection meetings where candidates are quizzed on how many meetings they attended in the last year. Both the Tories and the Liberal Democrats do not stipulate that candidates have to be members, although it probably helps. However, every four years each Councillor faces re-selection and both their ward and the Local Government Committee (in the case of the Labour Party) can de-select them. Even then, the choice of the local political party may not necessarily echo the preferences of the electorate.

Officers and Gentlemen

Local government is full of transvestites, members who want to take control of detail and officers who want to make policy.

Anon

Local government officers form the bureaucratic element of local democracy and have been in existence, in one form or another, for centuries as part of the machinery of municipal or parish government. Now they entail costs as high as half a local authority's total expenditure in any given year. Local government remains a major employer, with 2.1m of the British workforce working for local authorities (compared to a Civil Service of 500 000). These employees range from school cleaners through to chief executives, with, inter alia, social workers, teachers, admin staff and planning officers in between.

However, this number has been scaled back from the post-war collectivist period's peak of 3m, following the transferral of functions into the Quango state and the private sector (in the case of blue-collar employees). As the title of the chapter suggests, the gender profile of management in local government is biased towards men and an examination of the statistics suggests that the perception of local government officers as white middle-aged men remains justified, in spite of the fact that the strength of women in the local government workforce is at 70%:

Percentage of senior management posts in local authorities in England and Wales occupied by women for each of the top three tiers of management at April 2001, %:[44]

Chief Executives	12.1
Chief Officers and Directors	15.5
Deputy Chief Officers, Assistant Directors and Heads of Service	25.3
Total	23.0

Percentage of senior managers in local authorities in England and Wales from an ethnic minority group for each of the top three tiers of management at April 2001, %:[45]

Chief Executives	1.9
Chief Officers and Directors	1.2
Deputy Chief Officers, Assistant Directors and Heads of Service	2.0
Total	2.0

Percentage distribution of local government employees and those in the broader economy by age group in England and Wales, Spring 2001, %:[46]

	Local govt	Whole econ.
Under 25	6.1	15.3
25 -34	18.8	25.7
35 - 44	29.7	25.9
44 - 54	31.9	21.5
50 +	13.6	11.5

The 'glass ceiling' therefore is certainly no stranger to local government. However, the number of female chief executives and senior managers is rising rather than remaining static, with London Boroughs leading the way.[47] As far as the law is concerned, there are a number of posts that a local authority is required to have: a 'Head of Paid Service' (more commonly known as Chief Executive), a 'Monitoring Officer' (to ensure the Council's activities remain within the law) and a 'Chief Finance Officer' (who is usually the County or Borough Treasurer/Director of Finance), as well as an array of specialist chief officers such as Director of Social Services, Returning Officer (for elections) and Education Officer.

Beneath the senior management tier is the specialist tier of policy officers, IT professionals etc., and, more traditionally, lawyers and personnel officers. In addition to this there are a number of professionally qualified 'frontline' staff such as teachers, social workers, planners, environmental health inspectors etc. Most in number are the 'ATC' (administrative, technical and clerical) staff who are engaged in work such as school clerking and nursery nursing, and the blue-collar staff employed to sweep streets, empty bins and look after parks etc. The recent move towards 'Single Status' has broken down these artificial divisions to a difference between what are considered 'frontline' or support staff.

Broadly-speaking, the role of senior local government officers is to represent the interests of the local authority externally, manage staff and resources, and support and advise elected members.[48] We will concern ourselves with the role of officers in terms of providing support to elected members and the issues that arise as a result of this. Because Councillors are generally amateur politicians and not gifted with administrative skills (nor present in the town hall all of the time), the responsibility to work up strategies for the local authority falls upon officers, with the Councillors' role being to make political decisions around this. The nuances of this vary from authority to authority, with one extreme being the member-led authority and the other as an officer-led authority, although most are found in between the two as would be expected.

Additionally, through the use of delegated powers, officers are able to take major decisions affecting the local authority in terms of spending or granting permission on items such as licensing and planning. In all of this there is a certain amount of trust entailed but ultimately accountability is present through the fact that officers are hired and fired on the basis of their performance.

Officers play an integral role in political decision-making, meeting with Councillors to provide advice and guidance and writing committee reports and agenda items. The proceedings of the Widdicombe Committee in 1986 were concerned to some extent with not only the relationship between elected members and officers, but also the conduct of officers politically. Because senior officers enjoy a level of close proximity to and influence over elected members (who are likely to defer to specialist knowledge) there is a case for ensuring that senior officers are impartial and open partisan activity on their part will detract from this. This is said to maintain the confidence of both elected members and the public.

However, the Widdicombe Committee noted that a certain amount of 'twin-tracking' was taking place in local government, particularly in Labour local authorities during the 1980s. 'Twin tracking' was whereby senior officers in one authority also held political office as a Councillor in another and under this climate it was possible for appointments to be made on a partisan basis using internal party networks. Therefore the 'Widdicombe Ban' in the Local Government and Housing Act 1989 prevents all local authority officers above pay scale PO4 (or those involved in committee administration) from holding elected office as a

Councillor, holding an elected position (even in a voluntary capacity) in a political party or publicly declaring support for a political party through either canvassing or publication.

To most people this would appear eminently sensible; after all, elected members are dependent on the impartial advice given to them by officers. In exchange for losing their political rights, officers have the permanency that politicians do not as they are dependent upon election. However, this restriction also applies to political support staff for Council leaders and party groups, which appears somewhat unfair given that they do not enjoy permanency and are appointed purely for partisan reasons. It can be no coincidence that these posts were most common in Labour local authorities before the legislation was introduced, although there were profligate abuses such as Derek Hatton's serving as Deputy Leader of Liverpool while on a highly paid part-time consultant's contract for neighbouring Knowsley Council, and Walsall Council's stipulation that only officers with views "akin to Labour philosophy" could be appointed to senior posts. By and large though, the measure was, at worst, a sledgehammer to crack a nut or, at best, an aspirin in search of a headache. An interesting example of the politics concerned in the role of the officer nonetheless.

The new forms of executive governance in local authorities, with rationalised internal management structures and 'Cabinet' style government, have led to a more 'hands-on' style by Councillors of late and as a result of them becoming more full time they are able to micro-manage to a greater extent, although the dynamic between members and officers remains guided by the principles that prevailed under the committee system. It remains to be seen if this alters as the new forms of governance take effect and they may merit a more formalised role of officers in the decision-making process itself.

5 Local government and New Labour

Introduction – Mods and Wreckers

Local Councils exist to serve and speak up for local people. They can only do that properly if they keep in touch with local people and local organisations.[49]

New Labour may see local government as irredeemably linked to the past, as a theme park of Mayors' chains, inefficiency and producer politics.[50]

Following the 1992 General Election defeat, both the Labour Party and its satellite think tanks had generated a raft of policies concerning local government to bring into power with them at the next election. In particular, John Smith's brief period as Labour Leader was marked by the party's newfound interest in constitutional reform (or 'democratic renewal' to give it its New Labour buzzwords), previously dismissed as a chattering class issue under Neil Kinnock's time as Leader. In a marked contrast to the early and mid-1980s' rhetoric of municipal socialism with a new left edge, these policies were cloaked in a more managerial outlook.

Rather than just accepting Labour's recently acquired position of strength in local government, the language was largely concerned with Councils becoming more responsive to local communities and forcing local authorities to act more responsibly with their resources. Issued in 1995, the year that New Labour reformed the party's ideological article of faith, Clause IV, and made major electoral advances in the local elections of May that year, the policy paper renewing democracy, rebuilding communities. had a more anodyne air about it than anything else but was bold on the democratic leadership role – "a duty to promote the economic, social and environmental wellbeing of communities".

Outside of the conventional policy process in the party, however, ideas were fermenting such as adopting Michael Heseltine's fondness for directly elected Mayors. The intake of the 1997 Parliament, where Labour obtained its first Parliamentary majority for almost two decades, was characterised by an abundance of former Councillors and local government leaders. Far from being a trite observation, as is often the case in so many matters, the election of the 1997 Labour government was significant in terms of ending an era of British political history, as Young and Rao argue: "Local government in Britain has been treated throughout the postwar period as an instrument of central purposes. Councillors and officers were happy to go along with this, as implementing national policy meant growing budgets, staff and prestige. When expansion ended, the cutbacks that followed hurt badly. Redefining the place of local government in the political constitution was all the more painful."[51]

For Peter Latham of the Labour Campaign for Open Local Government, which sprung up as the last redoubt of municipal socialists, Labour's local government modernisation agenda is nothing more than "the latest step in the rollback of local democracy",[52] thus suggesting a continuation in the process embarked upon by Thatcher rather than a new era of localism. A narrative does exist however, for New Labour's modernisation agenda and this chapter will attempt to underline the thinking behind it. The party's 1997 manifesto, *Because Britain Deserves Better*, stated:

Local decision-making should be less constrained by central government, and also more accountable to local people. We will place on Councils a new duty to promote the economic, social and environmental well-being of their area. They should work in partnership with local people, local business and local voluntary organisations. To ensure greater accountability, a proportion of Councillors in each locality will be elected annually. We will encourage democratic innovations in local government, including pilots of the idea of elected Mayors with executive powers in Cities.[53]

At face value, the government has already achieved much of this agenda in its first term. The duty of local authorities to "promote the economic, social and environmental well-being of their area" was encapsulated in the Local Government Act 2000, as was the commitment to allow people to opt for directly elected Mayors, although the take-up rate for these has been slow. The desire for Councils to "work in partnership with local people, local business and local voluntary organisations" has been achieved through the implementation of Local Strategic Partnerships, whereas the use of Public Service Agreements has enabled them to pilot new freedoms under the concept of 'earned autonomy', buzzwords more synonymous with New Labour than any other. One of the first acts of the Blair government in 1997 was to sign the European Charter of Local Self-Government, which the Tories had refused to sign since it was written in 1985 (see Appendix I). A symbolic gesture, it does nonetheless affirm New Labour's recognition of local government's constitutional footing.

New Labour has not been willing to countenance the idea of a Power of General Competence, despite New Labour figures such as Margaret Hodge MP advocating such a move in her Fabian pamphlet, albeit just before Tony Blair's election as Labour Leader in 1994, when she wrote "A power of general competence would not mean a free for all with no central limits; what it would do is enable a local authority to act except where there was a specific provision."[54]

Change has been forthcoming in a number of other directions however, including the financing of local government and in particular the use of private finance in investment and modernisation schemes locally. Under New Labour there has been a massive expansion in the 'Governance Industry' as 'devolved agencies' spearheading new government initiatives and firms of consultants are formed in order to work on the government's policy agenda, particularly in regeneration and local democratic reform. Not a week seems to go by without another new think tank devoted to 'strategic thinking on the ground' being launched.

Much has been made of the presence of former Councillors and former Council leaders among the amassed ranks of New Labour at Westminster, perhaps leading some to hope that once in power, the party would be far from over for local government under New Labour. In reality, the inheritance bequeathed to New Labour was not in any kind of fit state to let that happen. The proliferation in the number of Quangos under the Tories, widely held to be a 'bad thing' in terms of their poor accountability, is an oft-cited aspect of the 'assault on local democracy'. However, some felt that local government had allowed itself into this position; "Local government was vulnerable to attack partly because of real weaknesses in its performance and accountability" was one view.[55]

The economic conditions of the 1970s had rendered local self-government an expensive luxury; it is no coincidence that the increase in local government's powers had taken place during periods of economic growth. From hereon in, governments had sought to curb local government expenditure and had imposed several financial straitjackets upon its operations. One analysis argued that local government had in fact been in decline since the 1940s[56] and given the gradual removal of its responsibilities for health and end of municipalisation (such as the transferral of local authority bus companies into the private sector) this is hard to dispute.

Also, the role of the 'loony left' Councils of the 1980s cannot be understated in terms of the evolution of New Labour thinking on local government. Most people's contact with an elected politician is not with the Members of Parliament or senior Labour figures that may be familiar to them through television and the press, but their local Councillor with whom they are engaged in matters of immediate relevance to them such as their local area of child's education. Therefore the scope of New Labour and the Millbank machine to sculpt the image of local Councillors or ensure they remain 'on message' at all times is rather more limited than it is with an MP.

By 1997, the Tories were regularly employing the electoral bogeyman of the 'Winter of Discontent' as part of their national strategy to fend off New Labour, with its images of rubbish piling high in Leicester Square and the backlog of unburied dead giving testimony to the dangers of left-wing extremism in local government (in spite of the fact that many of the Councils affected were in fact Tory gains of the late 1970s). Measures such as Compulsory Competitive Tendering (CCT) had the effect of curbing the power of the public sector unions and although Labour opposed CCT in principle, it did not want to give rise to new militancy in local government. The 'loony left' tag, should it ever return, would severely hamper New Labour in its attempts to woo Middle England, most Daily Mail readers having no time for local 'rainbow coalition' politics.

The cumulative effect of all these on the New Labour psyche was tremendous, from Neil Kinnock's landmark Bournemouth Conference speech in 1995 attacking Hatton's Liverpool for sending out redundancy notices by taxis through the mid-80s' excesses of Brent, Lambeth and Haringey to the stream of convictions in 'Donnygate' in the 1990s. The policy agenda was steeped in managerial constructs and any signs of nascent loony left activity were stamped out immediately, such as the case of Walsall Metropolitan District Council in 1995.

The Labour Council in the West Midlands elected left-winger Dave Church as its leader in May 1995 and his Radical decentralisation proposals were quickly seized on by the Tories as evidence of New Labour's active connections to municipal militancy. The party hierarchy were quick to respond, sending Shadow Environment Secretary Frank Dobson round studios to admonish the Council and pledge that Dave Church and his supporters would be expelled from the Party, which was the eventual result of the disciplinary action against him and the Labour Group in Walsall. In terms of its own political culture, New Labour had begun to critically assess its own past performance rather than just apportion blame upon the Tories for the decline in local government as a political institution, as Messrs Dromey, Filkin and Corrigan argue in their Fabian pamphlet:[57]

> *Modernising local government does not imply that we did was*
> *wrong in the past – local government has made great achieve-*

ments over many years. It led to the improvement of our cities in the nineteenth century and made a major contribution to post war reconstruction. But in the '60s and '70s local government lost touch with its public's needs and values. It saw its role primarily as an employer of large numbers of people to deliver services to a passive population whose main task was to pay the rates. The concentration was very much on the views and interests of producers. ...No one spoke to the community.

Like so many areas of New Labour local government policy, this is a double-edged sword – recognising the contribution made by local Councils on one hand and laying down the law on the other.

All the reforming zeal in the world could not eradicate the spirit of the Tory local government reforms and despite the newfound adherence to managerial methods and notions of good governance, Labour had taken much of that spirit on board. The replacement of CCT with Best Value still retained an element of the 'contract culture' integral to the operation of CCT as a move away from the 'producer politics' of Labour's past into a more moderate view of the New Right's vision of local authorities as 'enablers' rather than providers in the traditional mould.

Again, the concept of 'partnership' (as opposed to forms of either municipal or outright private provision) comes into context, with local authorities being seen as overseeing a 'genuine mixed-economy' of local services. This 'Third Way' was present in the Party's 1997 manifesto when it said: 'We reject the dogmatic view that services must be privatised to be of high quality, but equally we see no reason why a service should be delivered [by local authorities] if other more efficient means are available."[58] The Party was conscious that many in its assembled ranks of local Councillors wanted to merely re-municipalise former Council-run services without question of value for money or quality, once Labour was in government nationally, and this was one way of suggesting that such cartes blanches would not be available.

On the other hand however, the Labour Party did not endorse wholeheartedly the minimalist view of Nicholas Ridley and the Adam Smith Institute, who argued that the only role of local Councils should be to meet once a year to set the Budget and hand out contracts to the private sector for the provision of local services, with the rest of the year presumably spent at civic fetes or expediting constituents' casework. But it sought some accommodation with the view that the Town Hall doesn't necessarily know best when it comes to the efficient delivery of local services, although the ideal non-Council provider was just as likely to be a local charity or co-operative as a profit-seeking private sector company.

Indeed, following the Tory CCT regime, a number of large companies specifically set up to compete for local authority business emerged. such as Onyx and Serviceteam, whereas the problems associated with Capita's handling of local authority Housing Benefit functions are well documented in the press. The New Labour approach however, eschews such free-marketeering and views the local state as a regulator, purchaser and provider rolled into one, although it has not been especially critical of private sector failure (cf. Housing Benefit and Council IT services). Above all, the strategic role of local government is prized above all others, as is visible in other areas of New Labour activity.

Aside from the noticeable expansion in the Quango state, the 'big story' of the John Major Tory governments in terms of local government was the massive reorganisation programme it embarked upon. The expansion of the Quango state was certainly topical during this era and it drew a proportionate amount of criticism from Labour in opposition, although in government it did relatively little to reverse the situation. Even so, local government reorganisation, left by the Tories with many loose ends, was not a feature of Tony Blair's first term Labour government. The 'big story' under Blair has been the battle to coerce (and instruct if necessary) local government to become more responsive, accountable and prudent.

The new Department of the Environment, Transport and the Regions (DETR) 'super ministry', created to give Labour Deputy Leader John Prescott a department statuesque enough to placate his ego and indulge his predilection for regional government, had a busy time during the first term, occupied as it was with the legislation for the Greater London Authority, Best Value and elected Mayors, with distractions looming in the form of regional devolution.

The over-arching theme or metanarrative for this was 'modernisation' (this having enjoyed unrivalled currency in New Labour in most other policy areas) and all initiatives went under an umbrella of 'Modernising local government'. The government issued six consultation papers during this period, concerned with either management or finance, the concepts that were as at home under Thatcher and Major in terms of local government. The papers were:

- Improving local services through best value
- Local democracy and community leadership
- A new ethical framework
- Improving local financial accountability
- Capital finance
- Business rates.

The flavour of the papers displayed some degrees of willingness to embrace and foster radical change in local government management and structures, and a more cautious approach in terms of finance.

The attachment to high standards of probity found in the new Code of Conduct for Councillors and the creation of the Standards Board is a product of heightened awareness of 'sleaze' and corruption in public life during the 1990s, albeit at national level (this was 30 years after Poulson).

The re-appearance of the Dame Shirley Porter 'homes for votes' case in the House of Lords and the 'Donnygate' expenses scandal in the Yorkshire Labour stronghold of Doncaster were timely reminders that Labour in local government wasn't immune from scandals of its own and certainly gave impetus to the introduction of a national allowances framework for Councillors.

Labour's provincial hinterlands, particularly in the Northeast, had become increasingly vocal in demanding regional government and while devolution to Scotland and Wales had kept the government busy for the initial stage of the first term, the plans for elected regional government were subject to a tug-of-war between the DETR and Downing Street. Thus, the status of the remaining two-tier Councils in the English Shires was never fully assured and this may have clouded the waters to some extent.

The modernisation agenda was characterised by the 'carrot-and-stick approach' to many extents, the repeal of some unpopular policies (e.g. capping and CCT) but an enhanced duty to perform to centrally formulated targets. Local government was to be no exception to the revolution in service delivery and the government's approach in other areas (see below) was also fit for local government:[59]

- the notion of 'joined-up government', implying a seamless web of public services
- public-private partnerships to generate effective service delivery
- an emphasis on actual outcomes as they affect the citizen, rather

than on traditional outputs such as new legislation or ministerial directives.

While local authorities were treated more considerately than under the Tories, they did not receive much in the way of extra money from Whitehall in the first two years or a return of the powers whittled away from them over the preceding 20 or so years. Accusations of centralisation have inevitably been banded around on a regular basis, although not all Councils have resisted the agenda and some have been noted for their willingness to embrace it wholesale.

New Labour's approach has often been seen as a critique of local government and it has certainly shown a willingness to bypass local authorities, such as the extra funding directed straight to schools rather than to LEAs. It certainly views local government as one of several agencies on the ground capable of delivering its agenda and shows no ideological preference to retain local government in any position of pre-eminence in service delivery. Initiatives such as Education Action Zones are guided by principles and policies directed from Whitehall rather than by local Councillors in committee.

Much of the performance agenda has been stipulated directly by 10 Downing Street. Tony Blair and his burgeoning coterie of advisers ensconced in Number 10 had no intention of indulging the 'Old Labour' ways in local government and Blair sought to apply a new civic purpose to local government, reviving the tradition of local pride and dynamism in the Council Chamber. Having never been a Councillor, Blair's view of local democracy was largely fashioned by his experience of 'Old Labour' Councillors in his Northeast constituency or the media reports of Labour's activities during the 1980s, even going so far as to share the view of the many who simply don't bother to vote in local elections that Councils are unresponsive and irrelevant.

The 'Old Labour' world of producer politics and amateurism in local government is a million miles away from what Blair is trying to achieve in terms of raising standards and reforming the public services. Similarly, the New Labour attachment to modernity, 'Cool Britannia' and the digital age does not mirror the superannuated ranks of local Councillors typified by the largely white, male and elderly people local Labour Parties are fond of selecting.

When the government, in its Modern Local Government White Paper of 1998, attacked "the old culture of paternalism and inwardness", it was speaking to its own Councillors. John Prescott claimed that the White Paper heralded "the rebirth of democratic local government" but views obviously differed on how this could be brought about. The Home Office-sponsored 'Cantle report' on community cohesion (2001) cited weak political leadership as one of the contributory factors to the recent race disturbances in Northern towns. The dynamic kind of leadership associated with Blair and New Labour is not to be found in most Town Halls, where length of service or factional domination is still quite often the prerequisite for elevation to the Council leadership.

Local political leadership – elected Mayors and cabinet government

> *The seriousness with which people, politicians and the electorate alike, treat local government figures will alter under the new Mayoral systems that will breathe new life into local democracy and challenge previous assumptions on political behaviour.*[60]
>
> Dave Sullivan and Andrew Stevens

Directly elected Mayors were, until recently, an alien concept in British local government. The term Mayor is misleading as most people associate Mayors with civic duties and Borough flower shows. Elected Mayors are ostensibly Council leaders elected directly by the local electorate, rather than their fellow Councillors.

It was the Tory Environment Secretary, Michael Heseltine, who first floated the idea in Britain, although his plans didn't come to fruition under the Tories, as history demonstrates. Heseltine's reforms were proposed on the back of the abolition of the disastrous Poll Tax – he was seeking nothing short of a revolution in local government, with a tier of Councils abolished and the moribund world of local democracy given a dose of modernity. He had in fact, mentioned the idea in passing in his book *Where There's a Will*, written during his exile from the government front bench in the late 1980s.

His vision had its roots in initiatives such as the Urban Development Corporations, bodies operating outside of the confines of elected local government and consisting of government-appointed people drawn from business etc, charged with rejuvenating England's inner cities. It also had a whiff of the Victorian municipal ideal of civic pride, with bold visionary figures taking charge of cities. What began as a Tory wet managerial proposal that found no favour within the Tories themselves became the flagship local government policy for New Labour. Following the 1998 White Paper *Modern Local Government: In touch with the people*, which, for Councils' future reference, set out New Labour's stall, many local authorities clamoured to introduce new executive arrangements in anticipation of the legislation which would make them compulsory.

By 'massaging' previous local government legislation, Councils were able to introduce limited executive and scrutiny regimes that moved away from the traditional committee system of local government that had in fact been in existence for not far off one and a half centuries. Opponents of the modernisation agenda in local government are able to speak reverentially of the old committee system, often getting dewy-eyed in the process.

The anti-modernisation Labour Campaign for Open Local Government even used a 60-odd year old quote from Harold Laski, himself paying tribute to a bygone age of local democracy, in their spirited defence of the committee system: "... on the whole, anyone who compares the quality of local government today with what it was one hundred years ago, cannot avoid the conclusion that... the committee system has proved itself. It stands, with the Cabinet and the modern Civil Service, as one of the fundamental English contributions to the difficult art of self-government..."[61]

Outside of the Council Chamber, however, those prepared to defend the committee system against the baying dogs of modernity were few and far between. Change was taken up readily, with most Councils adopting the Leader and Cabinet system in advance of their statutory duty to do so, but opinion was divided on more advanced reform.

Elected Mayors were driven through by Tony Blair with the kind of same determination Margaret Thatcher employed when trying to get radical policies past Tory traditionalists. John Prescott, Blair's Deputy and the Secretary of State responsible for the implementation of the policy, certainly showed no enthusiasm for them, leaving the matter in his Minister of State Hilary Armstrong's devoted hands.

Backbench opinion in the Parliamentary Labour Party was at best agnostic, with vocal proponents of the policy being equally as few in number as those defending the committee system. The leadership loyalist Labour affiliate union the AEEU even went so far as to campaign against the introduction of the legislation that paved the way for elected Mayors, perhaps in search of a policy it could oppose in order to assuage 'Old Labour' sentiment within its rank and file.

The last say, however, was to be had by local citizens themselves in a referendum in each local authority area, should consultation indicate the preference for one. Clement Attlee once remarked that the referendum was "a device so alien to all our traditions", but Blair had chanced his arm on issues such as Scottish and Welsh devolution, the Good Friday Agreement and the London Mayor and Assembly and won the argument in favour of reform by taking his case to the people.

The referendum was anticipated as being able to overcome opposition amongst the forces of conservatism in local government (in all parties), by appealing to voters' sense of replacing a worn-out system that held little interest to anyone, and would also have the effect of entrenching the system in law by popular mandate. To understand the rationale for Tony Blair's personal enthusiasm for elected Mayors requires an examination of the state Blair found local government in when he was elected Leader of the Labour Party in 1994.

Blair became an MP in 1983 when 'loony leftism' was in its ascendancy; Council leaders such as 'Red' Ted Knight and Linda Bellos of Lambeth, Derbyshire's David Bookbinder and (of course) the GLC's Ken Livingstone left an impression upon him. In Council elections, where turnout can be as low as 30%, factional leaders of less than Blairite pedigree can become Council leaders under the narrow franchise of the majority group on the Council, and the possibility of high profile left-wing Council leaders attacking a Labour government was far from appealing.

It was of no surprise that elected Mayors became one of the first local government modernisation measures touted by New Labour. In 1996, Blair met the columnist Simon Jenkins, who had acted as Chair of the Commission for Local Democracy, for an informal discussion on the merits of elected Mayors and in the first instance an elected Mayor for London became firm party policy overnight. One of the other features that attracted Blair to directly elected Mayors was their appeal to those outside of the political system, although not the maverick left-wing populist they ended up with in the form of Ken Livingstone.

Popular local figures and business leaders could take charge of the inner cities and control local authorities without having to rely on being elected from amongst a Council's ruling party group. It isn't too hard to see why Blair was so attracted to the idea. The Labour Party's former Assistant General Secretary Matthew Taylor argues that the origins of the Mayoral agenda arose from New Labour's realisation that local Councils weren't going to put their own houses in order: "I think where it came from was desperation over the state of Labour local government. It was driven, and still is driven, by the need to improve the talent and quality of decision-making in local government. So I think the commitment to Mayors was in a sense a negative reaction."[62]

The arguments set out by New Labour in favour of elected Mayors tend to be based on the premise that direct election by the people means more democracy in the town hall and that Mayors would be Viagra for the flaccid institution of local government. Again Matthew Taylor argues that the base instinct was more concerned with local government being made to shape up: "There has always been in New Labour a pretty profound disdain for local government, for the current quality of local government. Part of that is rooted in the fact that throughout the 1980s the Conservatives were able to get quick wins out of loony leftism and all that stuff."[63]

So, we can take the need for better quality decision-making in local government and New Labour's fondness for people outside of conventional politics such as businessmen being able to bypass the normal entry route into local political leadership as being major factors in the ardent championing of elected Mayors. Until the first set of Mayoral elections that is.

The referendum on the Mayor of London (tied into a referendum on a new London Assembly) was the first test for Blair's policy on elected Mayors. The Tories stood by their decision to abolish the GLC and for obvious reasons were not in favour of the return of capital-wide government for London. However, despite their initial opposition when the plans were first mooted, the Tories had come round to the idea of an elected Mayor of London, just not the Assembly that was needed to hold the Mayor to account. Ken Livingstone remarked that most Labour MPs thought the plans for an elected Mayor were "absolutely barmy", but he voted for it anyway.

The necessary legislation was piloted through Parliament by Nick Raynsford, the Minister for London and an all-party 'Yes' campaign set up by London Labour luminaries Toby Harris, Margaret Hodge and Trevor Phillips, as well as longstanding Mayoral advocate Simon Jenkins and a handful of London Tories, who were blowing hot and cold on the issue. The Lib Dems, true to form, opposed the plans for a Mayor, as it would detract from their ideologically pure notion of pluralism. Not that it mattered as, in the 7 May referendum, 72% of the 34% who actually turned out to vote opted for the Mayor and Assembly of the new Greater London Authority.

The process, from legislative passage through Parliament to the referendum itself, actually paled into insignificance by the pantomime that followed in terms of the selection of Mayoral candidates by the political parties. The selection of Susan Kramer and Darren Johnson of the Lib Dems and the Greens respectively propelled two complete political unknowns into supporting roles, as both Labour and the Tories dithered over the selection of their candidates, with Jeffrey Archer falling from grace spectacularly.

The internecine debacle over Labour's last minute reversion from 'One Member, One Vote' to an arcane electoral college brought obscure aspects of Labour's constitution and its manipulation by the shadowy Millbank machine into people's front rooms through the relentless media coverage devoted to the contest between Ken Livingstone and Frank Dobson. When Ken Livingstone lost the selection but took the Mayoralty as an Independent candidate in May 2000, Londoners could have been in no doubt as to who was in charge of their City. Elected Mayors had arrived.

Ken Livingstone was a temporary setback for Blair's Mayoral project. Livingstone had, against the odds, taken on the control-freakery of the Millbank machine and captured the sympathies of Londoners of all classes and political allegiances. Opinion polling showed a strong preference among the public for the idea of being able to choose who runs their local authority directly[64] and the media became an active supporter of the concept, not least for the copy-generating function it had provided in London, with the Daily Express stating "We need to find a way to make City governance more attractive once again, and to reconnect voters with local government. The answer lies in directly elected Mayors."[65]

Elected Mayors did, however, remain a minority taste within the Labour Party and indeed the Labour government. They were not at home with the 'politics as usual' approach favoured by many at Westminster and in the political parties and had proven that some politicians could break free from the grip of party managers. The

Mayoral idea was associated with the modernising tendency within the Labour Party, those who were itching to tinker with the constitution in all kind of weird and wonderful ways, demanding proportional representation and decentralisation.

Shortly before Labour was elected in 1997, Labour MP Margaret Hodge and academics Steve Leach and Gerry Stoker published a Fabian pamphlet calling for the introduction of elected Mayors in local government. At the time, many thought that the idea would only take off in the main provincial cities; after all if London had a Mayor then Birmingham, Manchester and Sheffield wouldn't be far behind in the queue, followed by Leeds and Liverpool.

However, Hodge, Leach and Stoker called for Mayors in all Councils, citing the gravitas a Mayor would command compared to an ordinary Council leader: "We need strong local leaders providing community leadership for their areas. We want strong personalities with political weight. We want them to be influential so they can take on ministers and MPs and provide an effective balance to the centralised structure we have at present."[66] Following the White Paper of 1998 came the Local Government Bill 1999 (although it was August 2000 before it became an Act due to the Lords delaying over the repeal of Section 28, which was later dropped from the Bill), which set out the process for the introduction of new political arrangements in local authorities.

Under the Local Government Act 2000, local authorities must consult their citizens on the question of which model they prefer for the executive arrangements of their Council:

• Leader and cabinet
• Directly elected Mayor and cabinet
• Directly elected Mayor and Council manager.

If a majority of respondents in the statutory consultation indicate a preference for either of the Mayoral options, a referendum must be called by the Council on the issue. Voters are then asked if they agree with the Mayoral option or the 'fallback position' (which is agreed by the Council and is either the leader and cabinet system or the 'revamped committee' system). Similarly, a referendum can be triggered by a petition of 5% of the electorate in a local authority area or if the Secretary of State requests that one be held. Should the Mayoral options receive 50% or more (singularly or in total) in favour among the responses received in the statutory consultation, the Council is obliged to (in theory) hold a referendum on whether or not to have a directly elected Mayor in that authority.

Needless to say, this was not especially popular with many Councillors, the Labour Campaign for Open Local Government being set up to counter the Mayoral agenda and agitate for more traditional models of municipal socialist activity. Many Councils pressed ahead with the leader and cabinet system, the London Boroughs of Hammersmith and Fulham and Lewisham 'piloting' the arrangements two years before the Act took force.

The New Local Government Network, set up in 1997 and chaired by ardent Mayoral advocate Professor Gerry Stoker, established an intimate relationship with the Labour government, lobbying assiduously for modernisation (under the bracket of 'new localism') and campaigning for Mayors locally.[67] Whether or not Councils actually wanted Mayors was beside the point as far as the government was concerned, local people would have the last word.

Even those Councils in which the public rejected Mayors in either consultation or a referendum would still have to replace the committee system with a form of focused executive governance with a leader and cabinet system enforcing an executive/scrutiny split in the work of Councillors, with those in the cabinet/executive becoming virtually full-time service leads while backbenchers were now free to become 'frontline Councillors' and community champions by virtue of the reduction in hours they were required to put in at the town hall.

The proponents of elected Mayors, such as the New Local Government Network, argue that they would provide focused political leadership, increased political relevance and the gravitas and mandate to get the job done. The detractors of the Mayoral model, such as dissident Labour Councillors, the Lib Dems and Tory traditionalists, argue that an elected Mayor would be in effect a dictator with no means of impeachment between elections, unlike conventional Council leaders.

The Mayoral advocates claim, however, that the new system will be more democratic as it removes the power to select who runs the Council from caucuses within the ruling party group and transfers it to the electorate at large. Both the government and the Mayoral lobby pinned their hopes on a successful first airing for local authority elected Mayors being held on a 'Democracy Day' or 'Super Thursday', where Councils across the country would hold referendums on this burning issue of local importance.

However, poorly constructed legislation and a General Election delayed this and in the end, only a handful of local authorities actually opted to hold referendums and even then for many this was an opportunity to bury the issue for a few years and stick to what they knew. The government had envisaged the next stage of Mayoral referendums to be held in the big cities such as Birmingham, Manchester and Newcastle. However, the Councils that gave the issue its initial outing in public were the less than glamorous Watford, Hartlepool, Sunderland and Doncaster.

Mayoral referendum results to date

Council	Date	Result	For	Against	Turnout
Berwick-upon-Tweed	June 7 2001	No	3,617	10,212	64%
Cheltenham	June 28 2001	No	8,083	16,602	31%
Gloucester	June 28 2001	No	7,731	16,317	31%
Watford	July 12 2001	Yes	7,636	7,140	25%
Doncaster	Sept 20 2001	Yes	35,453	19,398	25%
Kirklees	Oct 4 2001	No	10,169	27,977	13%
Sunderland	Oct 11 2001	No	9,593	12,209	10%
Hartlepool	Oct 18 2001	Yes	10,667	10,294	31%
Lewisham	Oct 18 2001	Yes	16,822	15,914	18%
North Tyneside	Oct 18 2001	Yes	30,262	22,296	36%
Sedgefield	Oct 18 2001	No	10,628	11,869	32%
Middlesbrough	Oct 18 2001	Yes	29,067	5,422	34%
Brighton and Hove	Oct 18 2001	No	22,724	37,214	32%
Redditch	Nov 8 2001	No	7,250	9,198	28%
Durham City	Nov 20 2001	No	8,327	11,974	29%
Harrow	Dec 7 2001	No	17,502	23,554	26%
Harlow	January 24 2002	No	5,296	15,490	37%
Plymouth	January 24 2002	No	29,559	42,811	40%
Southwark	January 31 2002	No	6,054	13,217	11%
Newham	January 31 2002	Yes	27,263	12,687	26%
West Devon	January 31 2002	No	3,555	12,190	42%
Shepway	January 31 2002	No	11,357	14,435	36%
Bedford	February 21 2002	Yes	11,316	5,537	16%
Newcastle-under-Lyme	May 2 2002	No	12,912	16,468	32%
Oxford	May 2 2002	No	14,692	18,686	34%
Hackney	May 3 2002	Yes	24,697	10,547	32%
Stoke-on-Trent	May 3 2002	Yes	28,601	20,578	28%
Mansfield	May 3 2002	Yes	8,973	7,350	21%
Corby	Sep 26 2002	No	5,351	6,239	31%
Ealing	Dec 12 2002	No	9,454	11,655	10%

The first referendum, triggered by a petition gathered by a disaffected local would-be politician, in Berwick-on-Tweed alongside the June 7 General Election, provided a shaky start, with the electorate voting the idea down. Similarly, in Cheltenham and Gloucester the thumbs down was delivered by voters, spurred on by local newspapers campaigning for the retention of the towns' civic Mayors.

Watford was the first local authority to deliver a Yes vote, saving Blair's flagship policy from electoral oblivion and this was closely followed by Doncaster's affirmative vote, arguably coming on the back of both well-publicised local municipal corruption and a strong media presence from outgoing New York Mayor Gulliani after September 11.

The 'Gulliani effect' did not hold sway however, as October 18's 'Democracy Day' of six referendums (Brighton and Hove, Hartlepool, Lewisham, North Tyneside, Middlesbrough and Sedgefield) saw the idea knocked back in Blair's own constituency of Sedgefield and in the New Labour haven of Brighton and Hove, where former Council leader and would-be Mayoral candidate (Lord) Steve Bassam was perhaps too closely identified with the Yes campaign.

Subsequent referendums have shown a preference for the status quo, with only five out of 13 Councils opting for a Mayor. The Mayoral concept has so far not caught on in the big cities and those that have gone for the idea tend to have nondescript local identities in need of assertion (North Tyneside, Lewisham, Watford, Stoke-on-Trent) or negative image problems in need of dynamism (Hartlepool, Middlesbrough, Doncaster, Hackney) and perhaps this may have been a subconscious element in the voting behaviour in these admittedly low turnout affairs.

In a bizarre twist to events, Brighton and Hove actually regressed from leader and cabinet to a version of the old committee system following their referendum. An elected Mayor, together with recently obtained city status would have made Brighton the regional political power base of the Southeast outside of London, but the Council had decided that its 'fallback position' (the system voted for in the event of a No vote) should be the revamped committee system in order to make the choice in the referendum starker (as opposed to elected Mayor versus leader and cabinet). However, despite the presence of a New Labour political establishment in the city, its oft-cited libertarian green contingent won the day.

The lesson appears to be that the centre needs to let go – in both Lewisham and Middlesbrough the Labour Party has run into problems selecting candidates to the Mayoralty. In Middlesbrough, the unusually high turnout can be attributed to the campaigning done by Ray Mallon, the high profile controversial 'zero tolerance' policeman whose anticipated personal candidature made the referendum a personality issue rather than one of governance. The Lewisham troubles, however, have been connected to irregularities in the ballot between Dave Sullivan, the incumbent 'executive' Mayor, and his longstanding Labour group rival Steve Bullock.

Interestingly, only Lewisham and Middlesbrough saw high profile Yes and No campaigns emerge during their referendums, despite the government's anticipation that the issue would be debated at length across the country. However, the election of a football mascot ('H'Angus the Monkey') in Hartlepool and a maverick ex-cop in Middlesbrough, not to mention a Tory in North Tyneside, all seats Labour could normally win without even delivering a single leaflet, as Mayors has dampened any government enthusiasm for the idea and proven critics right to some extent. How these Mayors perform will be the acid test to gauge what mileage is left in the idea and how it will be applied in future. As two commentators remarked before the Local Government Act 2000 received Royal Assent:

> *Of course there are other forces at work which will determine whether cities thrive or decline, not least the role of culture and social entrepreneurship, as well as the obvious economic factors. Elected Mayors should be seen as part of a package of reforms, each*

unique to the particular circumstances of the geographical area, but each driven by the same need for democratic renewal.[68]

Not the only team on the pitch – Best Value

Elected Mayors struggled to stay part of the government's script during Labour's first term, with even Blair losing interest eventually. Best Value on the other hand was an integral element of New Labour's post-Tory approach to local government. It was patently evident that CCT had to go, the question was what to replace it with. To not replace CCT would have been bad management practice in New Labour's eyes, but it would also send out the wrong signs to the ranks of Labour Councillors who were hankering for its abolition. The key difference is that local authorities are no longer be obliged to put their services out to competitive tender but must demonstrate that they are obtaining Best Value for local people.

Some people have, of course, argued that the difference is merely one of semantics and wordplay. Best Value does reinforce an important ideological distinction that local authorities must work with other agencies in the public sector and the local private and voluntary sectors in the co-ordination of service delivery. Local authorities are 'not the only team on the pitch' – the essential differences between Best Value and CCT being that quality and reliability are as important as cost and that there should be a long-term collaborative partnership between the customer and service provider, not the previous rather adversarial relationship.

The role of competition has been reduced to management dynamic, rather than an obligation. New Labour did not want to deviate from the Tory approach of applying pressure to Councils to deliver efficiently and raise standards but it realised that the harsh perceptions of what CCT was intended to achieve had to be dispelled: "Achieving

Best Value is not just about economy and efficiency, but also about effectiveness and the quality of local services – the setting of targets and performance against these should underpin the new regime."[69]

The White Paper gave way to the 1999 Local Government Act and the operation of Best Value locally involves each local authority producing an externally-audited performance plan, a technocratic exercise which has been derided as a "management consultant's dream" by the Tories, although most local authorities have managed a painless transition to the new regime. The four main planks of Best Value, as outlined in the 1998 White Paper *Modernising local government – Improving local services through Best Value* are:

- targets, focused on the three Es – economy, efficiency and effectiveness
- annual performance plans, which must examine past performance and outline future plans
- new audit and inspections
- consultation with the public.

The aim was "to obtain best value by securing economic, efficient and effective services."[70]

Best Value has been derided by some traditionalist Labour Councillors as a centrally driven continuation of the erosion of local democracy (by tying Councillors' hands to some extent) but most Councils have shown a willingness to engage with it, being as it is the law of the land. It does not represent a complete departure from the principles of CCT but affords an increased degree of local flexibility. It also fits in well with New Labour's 'joined-up' approach to service delivery in order to achieve tangible results in the eyes of the public.

The framework for service provision is subject to supervision and standards set by central government whereas the local authority's role is to carry out Best Value reviews according to that framework. Council's must use the following criteria in their reviews (the 4 Cs):

- challenge
- compare
- consultation
- competition.

This allows for more flexibility than under the CCT regimes, although local authorities must still award contracts on the basis of fair and open competition. Many Councils have opted for a pragmatic approach, with a mixed economy of service provision using a mixture of in-house and private sector organisations. Diversity is strongly encouraged by the government; neither of the rigid models of service delivery favoured by the New Right or Old Labour find favour. In particular, many Councils rushed to privatise their Housing Benefit functions, with often disastrous effects. But services such as refuse collection and parks maintenance have been outsourced in many Councils without similar consequences.

In addition to Best Value, the government has introduced Beacon Councils as a means to encourage and share best practice. The government selects local authorities it considers to be performing exceptionally well and awards Beacon status to them for either a particular service or on their performance as a whole. This approach mirrors the government's use of 'raising and praising' in other areas of the public services.

The only show in town – PFIs and PPPs

It has been claimed that the reform of the public services represents the most important chapter in the history of New Labour and the use of private finance in Private Finance Initiative and Public Private

Partnership schemes is a major leitmotiv in that story. According to the Modernising Government White Paper, private finance has a role to play in the public services "not out of dogmatism, but out of pragmatism, because we want the best value for money". It is very emblematic of wider ideological distinctions between Old and New Labour as it symbolises the government's willingness to use the private sector in its plans to reform and improve public services.

The PFI owes its genesis to the Tories under John Major, although it was readily taken up by New Labour as a means to revitalise the public services. From CCT onwards, a role for the private sector in local services has been carved out by three successive governments under Thatcher, Major and Blair and a more private sector-orientated ethos has permeated many aspects of their operation as a result, regardless of whether services are delivered by the public sector (in-house) or private sector organisations (externalised). The client culture, derided a decade or so ago, is now accepted as the norm and in the main most Councils have accepted (albeit grudgingly in some cases) a role for the private sector in the delivery of services in a way acceptable to central government.

A source of tension between the centre and local Councils, the Thatcher and Major administrations were noticeable for the proliferation of Quangos (TECs for instance) and other devices designed to bypass elected local authorities in the delivery of services, and the use of the private sector is seen by some observers as the final phase of this process. Others, such as Councillors themselves, have been more pragmatic. Indeed, many Councils have been pioneering in their approach to working in partnership with the private sector and have worked off their own initiative in this area, albeit with strong central government encouragement.

The PFI, mockingly referred to as 'Pay For Infinity' by critics, was originally conceived by Norman Lamont (it was Lamont's successor

Kenneth Clarke who extended it to local government) in the early days of John Major's Conservative government as a means to underwrite major construction projects and improvements to infrastructure (the Chunnel rail link for instance) by using private sector finance. Such projects offer lower costs to the public purse and can often be built quicker than with using conventional public sector methods.

However, the crux of the scheme is that with the risk transferred to the private sector, its return has to be assured so therefore the private sector consortia involved in these schemes ensure a return through ownership of the facility in what are referred to as DBFO schemes (Design, Build, Finance, Operate). For instance, a hospital PFI in the NHS would see a hospital designed, built and operated using private finance by a consortia who would then lease the hospital back to the NHS, therefore with no deviation from the policy of free healthcare as the money changes hands between the state and the private sector. Similarly, a school's PFI would see a new school built by the private sector and run by the Governors with LEA-employed teaching staff but owned by the private sector who could then rent out the school's facilities in the evening and at weekends to increase the return on their investment even further.

Other local PFI schemes include the provision and maintenance of IT facilities in schools and the building and operation of leisure centres (the Downham PFI scheme in Lewisham is a combined library, pool and health centre operated by a number of agencies). The Local Government (Contracts) Act 1997 was an attempt by the new Labour government to get PFI up and running as its history up to that point had been particularly chequered due to legal worries and doubts about the nature of the contracts proposed. So far, local authorities have begun to accept the use of PFIs to introduce improvements to their capital projects in the absence of other resources.

The term Public Private Partnership has become more associated with the controversial proposals to part privatise the London Underground than anything else, but its another strand of the modernising approach and the use of the private sector in local government favoured by New Labour. These offer a degree of flexibility for local authorities in the use of private sector funding as they can take a number of guises and be used for a variety of purposes. In particular they have been used for economic development and regeneration, for the obvious purposes of the intrinsic interest the private sector would have in these areas, although the rationale behind many set up during Margaret Thatcher's time was to promote the concept of private sector involvement in urban regeneration in the spirits of the Development Corporations.

The partnership will usually be led by a local authority and may also feature a number of other public sector organisations, but all concerned are connected by a shared purpose. Furthermore, such partnerships can attract funding and investment from other sources such as the European Union, particularly if they address social objectives, and many partnerships have come into existence for this purpose alone. Some partnerships have been so successful that they have either been absorbed into government (Northern Development Company into its Regional Development Agency) or the private sector itself (Lancashire Enterprise PLC). Issues concerning accountability and the dilution of the role of locally elected decision-makers in the delivery of services stand out as the main criticisms of PPPs.

Both PPPs and PFIs continue to be controversial and their existence is certainly not welcomed by all involved in local government. Opposition from among the ranks of Labour Councillors is mounted by the Labour Campaign for Open Local Government, the last redoubt of those old enough to remember municipal socialism, with the same level of disdain for this New Labour policy as it has for directly elected Mayors. Furthermore, both main trades unions in local government, Unison and the GMB, have mounted high profile campaigns against the increased use of the private sector in local government.

Their interest is maintained through the debate on the conditions of staff that work in the schemes, as they are no longer local government staff once a facility is transferred into the PFI, although their literature suggests an altogether more political motive for opposition: "It is about who makes the decisions about caring for your elderly relatives or your children's education or housing the homeless – someone with their heart in the right place, or someone with an eye on the balance sheet."[71]

However, New Labour has staked a great deal on PFI and it remains a flagship policy in terms of reforming the public services at all levels of government and in all areas of service delivery. For local authorities though, it can mean the difference between a leaking state-owned school roof or a state of the art classroom leased by a consortium, and, ideological considerations aside, the implications for the voting public will be paramount at election times.

All aboard – Local Strategic Partnerships

Another major facet of New Labour thinking on local government has been the emphasis upon partnership working. Partnership working, often expressed through PPP for specific goals, has been adopted by the government in other areas of local services, such as education (Education Action Zones and Excellence in Cities initiatives) and health (Health Action Zones).

The drivers behind the creation of Local Strategic Partnerships (LSPs) were the problems faced by many urban local authorities in bringing together all of the principal actors (other public bodies, voluntary sector) in a locality in order to holistically maximise co-ordination and communication between them. In particular, the Neighbourhood Renewal agenda set by the Cabinet Office's Social Exclusion Unit stipulates their creation and recognition in the areas in which the Neighbourhood Renewal Fund operates.

As a tie-in with the new statutory community planning duty, Local Strategic Partnerships are meant to refashion local governance around all of the key players in a locality and are not meant to implement or deliver services directly, nor be dominated by the local authority itself. Their ultimate purpose is to link neighbourhoods to the strategic regional agenda and provide a forum for dialogue in the local public sector. LSPs build upon existing partnerships in local governance – Local Agenda 21, New Commitment to Regeneration etc – and incorporate representatives from the increasing number of organisa-tions in and around the 'Governance Industry' such as Connexions, New Deal for Communities and Learning and Skills Councils.

Their creation reflects the earnestly held desire for more local co-operation on the part of those engaged in the public services 'on the ground' and at first glance they would appear to be a common sense initiative to avoid over-duplication etc. They also fit into the new Neighbourhood Managers agenda (the process of rolling out Neighbourhood Managers as identifiable stewards of communities), enabling them to feed into the partnership the concerns and needs of neighbourhoods.

The first issue arises where areas are eligible for Neighbourhood Renewal funding and therefore the 'talking shop' nature of the LSP could lead to it being a distraction for all concerned. Critics of LSPs claim they are no substitute for proper local government, citing the usual arguments about accountability and transparency of decision making.[12]

Another criticism levelled at their creation is that they represent yet another top-down imposition on local government, with Councillors no longer being able to decide who they want and don't want to work with, while others doubt the level of genuine community involvement and participation that partnerships claim to promote.

Furthermore, too broad a partnership will lead to inertia through convolution, whereas a smaller partnership in terms of reducing the number of those invited to sit on it will be unrepresentative of the community. However, it has been pointed out, by the government mainly, that LSPs offer a voice to generally underrepresented groups such as black and ethnic minority organisations. Regardless of whether or not actual practice reflects this, LSPs are a opportunity for local government to become more 'joined-up' in the way that New Labour wants all of the public sector to be.

Conclusion – Rights matched by responsibilities

New Labour's attitude towards local government has been shaped by the Labour Party's previous experiences. The notion that Britain is a unitary state has long held sway and has affected the behaviour of political parties. Labour has always been keen to demonstrate that Labour Councils are efficient and responsive to local needs, even if one or two examples have detracted from this and tainted its image. However, as a party of considerable strength locally it could not point to national success in government and therefore party managers have long sought to distance themselves from disastrous episodes in the Party's history, of which local government has supplied a few.

Therefore it should have come as no surprise that New Labour did not give local authorities, of whom party managers have little control over except in the most extreme of circumstances, carte blanche to act on every whim that passed it by. nor granted it the powers taken away from by the Tories (very much in the same way it has not repealed Tory industrial relations legislation, despite the demands of its union affiliates).

Instead we have seen the managerial revolution that has been rolled out across the Civil Service extended to local government from Whitehall. Local authorities have not been immune from the attention lavished upon other areas of the public sector in the form of target-setting and inspection, with the activities of the Office for Standards in Education being extended to LEAs themselves, as opposed to just the schools they maintained, as was the case in the past. Furthermore, the emphasis has been upon local authorities obtaining 'earned autonomy' through a variety of means rather than just being content to accept any freedoms that Whitehall would be prepared to give them, not that this was forthcoming in any case. The new Public Service Agreements (PSAs) represent this agenda made flesh.

In the government's words they will "[set] out [a local] authority's commitment to deliver specific improvements in performance, and the Government's commitment to reward these improvements. The agreement also records what the Government will do to help the authority achieve the improved performance."[73] The 'something for something' nature of the agreements is limited purely to Councils the government feels are achieving results and showing a genuine willingness not only to deliver for local people but also to work within the agenda it sets for them.

For the rest, there is no change and only more inspections and targets to look forward to. In fact, the government's 2001 White Paper *Strong Local Leadership – Quality Public Services* proposes that Councils be banded in league tables and their performance rated *a la* the 'Michelin star' system, with badly under-performing Councils facing the possibility of ministerial administration or the transferral of their responsibilities to other bodies.

Critics of PSAs claim that they represent yet another attempt to micromanage local government from the centre and coerce resource-starved Councils to dance to New Labour's tune. However, the participating Councils have responded positively and sought to pilot PSAs constructively in a number of areas such as community safety, transport and housing.

Local government is in a state of perpetual change and this has been accelerated under New Labour. Its first term was characterised by extending the Heseltinesque technocratic style to all aspects of local governance – Cabinet government (whether through elected Mayors or the more traditional leader), Best Value, Local Strategic Partnerships, Beacon Councils and PFIs have all played a major part in this. However, we have also seen a return to the rhetoric of civic pride and local political leadership – key concepts in any bid to re-engage the governed with their governors, that most topical of challenges.

Local government is the most immediate interface that people have with elected politicians and it has not escaped Parliament and the Civil Service that local government is far from enjoying the levels of confidence and participation that it once enjoyed. At the same time, many Councillors feel undervalued and marginalised by the modernisation agenda. But the friction between the centre and local Councils that existed under the Tories has not been replicated to the same degree under New Labour and, in many, examples of genuine partnership between them can be easily demonstrated.

6 The regional dimension – a few words

At present English regionalism has few fans and only a few regions have a sufficient identity to sense a political culture of their own which aspires to representation. Elsewhere, England lacks clear regional identities and is, for the most part, too mobile to figure out what could constitute any boundaries.[74]

To attach the subtitle of 'a few words' to the subject of regional government is ambitious in itself, given that a few rainforests will have been cut down in the name of the welter of reports, papers and studies devoted to it. But we can try. The move to make the Office of the Deputy Prime Minister into a fully-fledged Department of State saw the responsibility for the regional affairs and local government brief transfer into it from the disaggregated and short-lived Department for Transport, Local Government and the Regions. Commentators likened to this a 'mini empire' for Deputy Prime Minister John Prescott.

Given both Prescott's fervour for regional government and the policy co-ordination role the department now plays, it is effectively a ministry for sub-national relations within England, the only nation in the United Kingdom not to have its own devolved government. Regional government was felt to be off the political agenda when the brief was transferred from John Prescott's Department of Environment, Transport and the Regions to Stephen Byers' DTLR following the June 2001 General Election.

Now, for the second time, the regional government brief is held by one of its biggest fans in government. Strictly speaking, regional government is concerned with devolution, the process of passing down powers from central government, and therefore local government does not enter into the equation until any regional governments are live and relations need to be established between the two.

However, while many of the most ardent proponents of regional government are to be found in local government itself, many of its detractors can be located there also and the logic behind the process of devolution is thought by many to be to local government's detriment, as we will see. On top of modernisation, it may yet become one of the big stories behind local government reform over the next decade.

The origins of regional government

Those demanding regional government for England began campaigning shortly after the 1992 General Election as a result of Labour and the Lib Dems' devolution plans for Scotland and Wales, with the argument that the Tories had no mandate to govern the North clearly having some resonance. Regional government has long been a totem demand of Labour's 'heartlands' and also one of other parties on the progressive left such as the Liberal Democrats and the Greens. The issue arose during the deliberations of the Kilbrandon Commission in the 1970s, whose report backed the idea of regional assemblies for England alongside the proposed devolved bodies for Scotland and Wales.

The Kilbrandon Commission on the Constitution was established in the late 1960s by then Labour Prime Minister Harold Wilson as a means of examining ways in which Scottish and Welsh nationalist sentiment could be placated, lest it have any electoral consequences for Labour in either of its two safe electoral berths. The Commission reported in 1973,[75] under Tory Prime Minister Edward Heath however. Initially the idea attracted some supporters amongst One Nation Tories such as Quentin Hogg and Kenneth Clarke and by the early 1990s Labour's hierarchy in the North was eagerly pushing the idea within the national party, with future Cabinet minister Alan Milburn penning a paper for the North-eastern regional Labour Party on the subject.

In 1994 the Tory government under John Major introduced a small measure of administrative devolution in the form of the Integrated Regional Offices (now renamed Government Officers of the Regions) that oversaw the work of the Civil Service in the provinces. The regional devolutionist cause became a mainstream component in the party's raft of constitutional reforms under John Smith's leadership, following Labour's acceptance of the constitutional reform agenda (previously dismissed as the concern of the chattering classes).

However, under Tony Blair's leadership the proposals were modified and the Party's 1995 policy paper *A choice for England* written by Jack Straw, a known sceptic of constitutional reform, stated that approval by a referendum in each region would be a condition of their creation. Very much an issue associated with groups such as constitutional reform pressure group Charter 88 (whom former Labour Leader Neil Kinnock dismissed as "Whiners, whingers and wankers"), the implementation of the policy ran into trouble in the Labour's first term; it was in fact one of the only two Manifesto commitments that the government unashamedly failed to deliver on or make any progress towards (the other being a referendum on proportional representation for the House of Commons).

The situation is the reverse of that regarding elected Mayors: Tony Blair is known to be sceptical (the Bill to pave the way for regional referenda took five years between the 1997 Manifesto and the 2002 Queen's Speech) whereas John Prescott, as we have seen, and what might be referred to as 'Old Labour' are generally enthusiastic, although the Prime Minister's view that they have little popular support outside of regions such as the Northeast and Yorkshire fits in well with opinion polling on the subject.

Organisations such as the Campaign for the English Regions and regional initiatives such as the Campaign for a Northern Assembly (who have kept the issue alive since 1992) have lobbied assiduously with the support of many MPs and Ministers and at times it has seemed that the government may move the agenda forward. However, the story of regional government during Labour's first term in office is merely concerned with the running out of long grass for Ministers to kick the issue into: " . . . the momentum behind regional government seems to be declining, with little progress in this area . . . constitutionally and practically, it may not seem a problem that the constituent parts of the UK have different forms of devolution."[76]

Both Labour (in terms of agreed party policy) and the Liberal Democrats remain committed to the introduction of regional government but with a decade's worth of blueprints flying around to base it on, the only remaining question appears to be, when? The creation of eight Regional Development Agencies (RDAs) outside of London as a result of the 1998 White Paper *Building Partnerships for Prosperity*[77] as a first stab at some kind of regional policy was taken as a step in the right direction.

Yet, alone, these are not any kind of regional government in the way that the regional lobby would like. Furthermore, the transfer of responsibility for their upkeep to the Department of Trade and Industry following the 2001 General Election was perceived as a retrograde step in terms of the devolution agenda, suggesting as it did that their purpose was business-orientated rather than political. A White Paper, *Your Region, Your Choice*, the title echoing the commitment to referendums on the issue, in May 2002 was one of the last acts of the erstwhile DTLR before it was disaggregated.

Regional government and its merits

To set the concept of regional government in context, we have to look at the evolution of the British unitary state over the past 300 or so years. In 1707 England entered into a union with Scotland, with the addition of its Irish territories in 1801 (Wales was already incorporated into England by 1707), thus concentrating government at Westminster. This is usually what is meant when the unitary state is referred to.

Here, we are not concerned with Angles and Saxons but the presence of the nation state. Now, however, we have entered an altogether different era, as the unitary state is no more. Scotland, Wales and Northern Ireland now enjoy, to different extents, substantial devolved powers and responsibilities. Furthermore, under the 'Good Friday Agreement', Northern Ireland not only enjoys devolved government but the framework of the British 'union' established in 1801 has an extra dimension through joint-relations on certain matters with the Republic of Ireland. England, though, remains for all intents and purposes governed by the Parliament at Westminster acting through the Civil Service in Whitehall, both of which co-exist in the same postal area of London.

Devolution is usually associated with the idea of 'Home Rule', which is in itself a throwback to the time of Gladstone. More recently, as we saw earlier, in the mid 1980s the Conservatives abolished London's strategic regional authority – the Greater London Council – as well as the Metropolitan Counties, these being essentially mini-regional authorities by virtue of their size alone.

The problem in most politicians' minds is that either term entails handing over power to another body and, regardless of where that body is located, you don't achieve power through the ballot box in order to give it away to another political institution elected through a different ballot box. Devolution to the English regions was very much a live issue a long time before Labour published its 1997 White Papers on devolution to Scotland and Wales. Moreover, the failure to bring forward plans for the English regions in the late 1970s saw a number of English Labour MPs come together in common cause with Scottish and Welsh anti-devolutionists.

Since then however, the idea steadily gained acceptance among both Labour MPs and the Party's rank and file, as "... after a considerable period of Conservative government... many parts of the country had suffered badly at the expense of London and the Southeast. Once in government, however, New Labour did not see the need to pander to its regional interests, and this reform was one of those conveniently slid onto the backburner by a sceptical Civil Service, occasionally being reheated by the promise of a Green Paper as a tantalising motivator for grassroots activists."[78]

While New Labour is reluctant and constantly side-steps the issue with due caution, there are clear and powerful arguments in favour of devolution. As long ago as 1973 (before the author's lifetime in any case), Lord Crowther-Hunt wrote what remains the most coherent and enduring case for devolution to the English regions in his Memorandum of Dissent to the Kilbrandon Commission:[79]

- Local government is too closely controlled by the officials of central government
- Over-centralisation produces too much uniformity, whereas the needs of the different parts of the UK are obviously very varied
- In the allocation of resources the special needs and wishes of the different parts of the UK are not properly appreciated
- Central government has now become so big and its attempts at administrative control so detailed that there is frequently a lack of co-ordination between the thousands of departmental officials
- The centre is seriously overloaded. Ministers are overloaded and have little time for long-term or even short-term policy thinking

The main arguments in favour of devolution are not concerned with pluralism (as some, the Liberal Democrats included, have argued), but the desire to see decision-making redistributed to the closest possible level, rather than politicians in Westminster making those decisions on behalf of people they do not represent or nationally-recruited Civil Servants determining policy for localities far removed from Whitehall. It is as much geographic as political.

In the spirit of this geographical realisation, we need to acknowledge that regional identities have been formed – whether it is through Tyne Tees, Yorkshire or Granada television or through travel to work areas. We rarely hear that centralisation is a 'good thing' politically speaking, except for when demands are made to tackle the latest 'postcode lottery', but much of what has occurred over the last quarter of a century in terms of government decision-making roughly corresponds to that. If Scotland and Wales, whose population levels put together do not even equal that of some of England's larger regions, can be afforded devolved government, then why not afford the benefits of this to the English regions (albeit in a more limited form)?

The Labour government itself has recognised that "decisions made at the regional level can take better account of the unique opportunities and challenges faced by an individual region."[80] The controversial 'Barnett formula' (so-named after it was introduced by Labour Treasury Minister Joel Barnett as a temporary measure in the late 1970s) demonstrates the financial irregularities in the British constitution under devolution; effectively tax revenues raised from populous and prosperous regions such as London and the Southeast are used to subsidise the UK Treasury's funding of Scotland and Wales (who contribute less tax revenues by virtue of their smaller populations) under this system, even in post-devolution Britain. Without regional assemblies to speak up for areas such as the Northeast and the Midlands, it is more than likely that this system will remain in place. At a more local level, the inability of local authorities outside London (who have traditionally suffered under financial settlements agreed by the government) to collectively lobby on a regional basis for increased funding from central government merely exacerbates this problem.

Some have pointed to the culture of government decision-making as making a firm case for devolution. The legislative practices of Westminster and the machinations of Whitehall do not lend themselves to balanced consideration of regional interests, say in the case of ship-building in the Northeast or tin-mining in the Southwest, two industries that have been destroyed with considerable social consequences as a result of lacking any kind of regional response at the time.

Others, such as former Cabinet minister Peter Mandelson, point to a reduction in bureaucracy (opponents of devolution claim it will increase it) as one of the main reasons for supporting regional government: "Regional assemblies will reduce the existing layers of government bureaucracy and avoid duplication that currently occurs when regional strategies cut across one another."[81]

This is the crux of why Westminster politicians are willing to take power in order to give it away, as without doing so leads to its own fair share of problems. At the end of the day, no one is proposing to grant the Northeast the same powers as Scotland or even the limited form of devolution in Wales. Even then, there are a number of caveats incorporated into the policy, such as the requirement for prior approval by referendum before any kind of regional assembly can take shape in any one area.

The powers of regional government, while enough to make a difference in localities, would not be sufficient enough to present a threat to central government, as the inability of London Mayor Ken Livingstone to stave off the part privatisation of London Underground has shown recently. In John Prescott the regional government lobby have found a friend and ardent supporter. As one commentator, the devolutionist Simon Partridge, has argued, there are far greater issues at stake if Labour continues to display reticence and reluctance to act on this policy commitment: "If Labour is to escape the suggestion that its moves to devolution in Scotland, Wales and Northern Ireland are more a response to a nationalist separatist agenda, rather than the modernisation of an over-centralised state, the present devolution asymmetry in the rest of England (apart from Greater London) must be no more than a temporary measure. However, if the asymmetry lasts for any length of time, far from leading to a stable constitutional settlement, it is likely to encourage nationalist separatism – certain to be clothed in the innocuous sounding language of 'self-determination' – including an English backlash."[82]

Regional government and its demerits

Of course, the idea of regional devolution doesn't sit well with everyone and for a myriad of reasons as well. Opposition to the regionalist agenda usually comes in one or more of three forms:

- The preference for and acceptance of the status quo, i.e. leaving devolved assemblies in place in Scotland and Wales and relying on Regional Development Agencies to deliver on any regional aspirations
- The 'Tory' critique of devolution – the legislative anomaly created by the Scottish Parliament vis-à-vis Westminster (West Lothian Question) means that an English Parliament not regional government is the answer
- The preference for 'City regions' as a means of creating urban powerhouses for regeneration in order to ameliorate intra-regional economic disparities.

It would appear that the first variant of opposition is shared by New Labour at the centre and some quarters of local government itself (most notably at County level, for obvious reasons). From the government's perspective, it is not hard to visualise why this is the case. To roll out a programme of regional devolution across England in the form of elected regional assemblies would represent a sizeable administrative exercise; to do this on the basis of little demonstrated demand beyond the aspirations of a vocal regionalist lobby would scarcely be in the government's interests. Secondly, devolution to Scotland, Wales and London has already opened several Pandora's boxes in terms of raising the English Question, the lack of outright control by Labour in its heartlands in these institutions and internal problems over the selection of candidates.

To replicate this in eight more areas could present not only its own set of problems but also set in train more demands for constitutional reform as a result of what is becoming an unbalanced constitutional settlement. New Labour feels content that elected regional government can only come about where demand is readily apparent and this is reflected in the series of anaemic White Papers[83] on the issue. Furthermore, unease among County Councillors on the issue risks dividing the ranks of Labour local government. Sceptics in the government cannot be blamed for thinking that they could be creating rods for their own backs. However, the idea does have considerable backing among MPs and Labour Party activists so the issue is not likely to go away should the status quo be considered to be the most viable option.

The Tory critique remains the concern of a few backbench Conservative MPs and the Campaign for an English Parliament, which is the antithesis of the Campaign for the English Regions both politically and in terms of the demographic make-up of its supporters. They argue that regionalism is an agenda set by Brussels as the proposed regions reflect the boundaries of the Standard Regions used by the EU in policy-making and to elect English Members of the European Parliament, with the concept as "little more than a bureaucratic exercise".[84] Opposition also stems from the fact that "Lines have been drawn on maps that take no account of where people's sense of identity or loyalty lies,"[85] suggesting to some extent that their opposition is in fact as much cultural as political.

The campaign, however, has little support beyond the Tory back-benches as many Tories feel that another tier of bureaucracy should be avoided at all costs, regardless of Scotland's Parliament. In all other respects however, the Tories remain implacably opposed to regional government as it not only creates more bureaucracy but would also install an alternative Labour power base in the North that could act as a mandated opposition to any Tory government at Westminster.

The mooted abolition of County Councils does not help the

regionalist cause in the eyes of the Tories either. There is also a modicum of good old-fashioned scepticism in there as well: "Regional government in England is not a high priority for the general public. The key issues are crime, health, transport, education and the environment. People want trains that run on time, not more politicians and bureaucrats,"[86] (taken from a 'Localis' press release).

In some quarters though, opinion appears to be shifting with the moderate Bow Group advocating regional devolution as part of new Tory thinking on achieving public service reform.[87]

City regions originate from the early days of the more recent push for regional government, beginning as it did with the formation of Charter 88 during the late 1980s. While campaigners felt that the Tories were becoming increasingly bereft of a mandate to govern those regions in the North where relatively few people had voted for them, some felt that our once great cities were in need of not only reinvigoration but also actual recognition as drivers of regional economies.

The model for city regions comes from the German cities in the North such as Hamburg and Bremen, which have their own Lander (regional governments) alongside larger units such as Bavaria and Saxony. In the early 1990s, commentators remarked that English regional devolution should proceed on a more organic locally-driven path, with each region deciding on its boundaries and powers, which could have led to the likes of Birmingham, Newcastle and Sheffield becoming regions in their own right alongside Yorkshire and East Anglia for instance.

To some extent, England had city regions until 1986 in the form of the Metropolitan Counties, e.g. Sheffield as South Yorkshire, Liverpool as Merseyside, Newcastle as Tyne and Wear, and so on. But the idea was more of a throwback to Victorian municipal expansionism in places like Joseph Chamberlain's Birmingham for instance. More recently, the idea has been dusted off by the New Local Government Network[88] as a way to combine local political leadership with a solution to the English Question that doesn't involve vast regional assemblies.

Dismissed by regional campaigners, the idea would have made for an interesting concept had regional devolution proceeded along the path that many in the early 1990s assumed it would once Labour were actually in power to do anything about it.

The impact on local government

Aside from possible rivalry and perceived prestige, from many local Councils' perspective, the reason why the idea of regional government is so controversial is the requirement for even more reorganisation. On one hand, many Labour Councillors, particularly at District level outside London, are actually part of the campaigning lobby for elected regional assemblies (for instance, many of the leading lights in the North East and North West Constitutional Conventions are Labour Councillors). On the other hand, County Councillors of both Labour and Tory affiliation are generally against the proposals.

These are very much seen as the first direct threat to the County tier of local government since the Local Government Reorganisation of the mid-1990s, fears voiced through organisations such as the County Councils Network when talk was made of the need for a predominantly unitary system of local government. The facts speak for themselves here: "Nearly 70% of the Northeast and the Northwest regions are covered by unitaries but this proportion falls to just 20% in the East Midlands and 12% in the East".[89]

In terms of a government view, they have made it explicitly clear – "regionalism means reorganisation", to quote one John Prescott[90] in 2001. The 2002 White Paper, *Your Region, Your Choice*, made good on this by reiterating the Labour Manifesto promise that directly elected regional assemblies would be created "where predominantly unitary local government is established".

The White Paper argues that "[elected assemblies] would comprise a third elected tier – region, County, district – below national government, and the Government recognises that this would be one tier too many.",[91] although it doesn't state why it would be "one tier too many" in terms of it necessarily being a bad thing – plenty of our European counterparts have three sub-national tiers; it is a particularly British aversion to 'Big Government' that is being pandered to. Furthermore, the proposals for unitary local government in those regions that do not already possess it would be worked up by the (local government) Boundary Committee and presented to voters alongside any referendum being held on an elected regional assembly, so, in essence, voters would be asked to decide not only on the issue of the assembly but also on the future shape of local government in that region.[92] So, 'Yes' would mean wholesale reorganisation and 'No' would leave the status quo in place.

Using an equation comprising the British psyche regarding change, apathy and the lack of demonstrated demand for regional assemblies, it would not be a difficult task to call which way some of the referendums that may be held could go, although some County Councils are already lobbying for unitary status.

If all goes according to the regionalists' plan then the first regional assemblies could open their doors for business after the next General Election, the first referendum being mooted for the Northeast in 2004. If so, the new unitary authorities will have to work in partnership with the regional assemblies, these possibly sharing a common membership unless the political parties prevent the 'usual suspects' from being selected. Once the assemblies are in place, it will be interesting to watch the dynamic between them and the local authorities beneath them, as partnership may not necessarily entail freedom from dissension or even conflict.

7 Conclusion – may you live in interesting times

The saying "May you live in interesting times" is thought to be an old Chinese curse (although its first documented use was in fact by Robert F. Kennedy in 1966) but it aptly describes the conditions under which local government in Britain exists today. We have seen how local government is an essential component of both national political life and a vital tool for the delivery of local public services, supplying as it does a representative role ('local Council') and a service delivery function ('local authority'). However, it exists at the behest of Parliament and quite often takes its orders from Whitehall. It has, as David Widdicombe argued, no independent right to exist.

It does, however, perform an important constitutional role in terms of diffusing power throughout the state and providing a local mechanism for representation and advocacy, as Widdicombe also maintained: "The case for pluralism is that power should not be concentrated in one organisation of state, but should be dispersed, thereby providing political checks and balances, and a restraint on arbitrary government and absolutism."[93] It provides a stable platform for local issues and represents an identifiable link between the citizen and the state, with its functions and duties having as much bearing on their life as any other aspect of governance.

As we have also seen, local government has long been felt to be underperforming by central government and undervalued by those it serves. As such, it is under relentless and immense pressure to 'modernise' both its services and culture, and become 're-engaged' with voters in order to halt the trend of ever-decreasing turnouts. To this end, central government (with some assistance and guidance from the forward-looking elements of local government) in the form of New Labour has devised, as we have seen, a number of measures and innovations with the purpose of delivering on that modernisation and changing the culture of local government.

Reforms such as Best Value, new executive arrangements, Local Strategic Partnerships, Beacon Councils, the Comprehensive Performance Assessment and Public Service Agreements are just several of the 'hoops' that New Labour has made local Councils jump through in order to satisfy it, perhaps dragging some of them and their Councillors along unwillingly at times. John Major was fond of saying that local authority expenditure had too much bearing on national spending and many in New Labour would agree with him.

So far the emphasis has been on quality of decision-making and value for money services; once it has got local government's house in order then it may decide to concentrate on purely financial matters. Furthermore, a partial revolution has already begun in this area and many have argued that local government is very much at the mercy of the Treasury's already considerable hold on government in this country. We cannot afford to overlook the Tories in terms of this analysis; after all they could be in a position to implement their plans for local government in the near future. But leaving the Tories and New Labour aside, local government's constitutional role has not been unaffected under the weight of these changes and consideration should be given to how it might change even further in future.

What future for local government as a political institution?

In spite of passing challenges and threats (it was rumoured that John Major's Cabinet once discussed the abolition of local government altogether), the continued existence of local government is assured. This is because, at the very least, there is no substitute for the 'on the ground' delivery of services being administered by locally elected representatives with a strong raison d'etre. Another reason is that local government occupies a constitutional position assured by history – elected local government came into existence alongside the reforms of Parliament in the Victorian age.

However, that is not to deny that there haven't been attempts to considerably curtail its activities and even airbrush troublesome elements out of existence altogether (the GLC and Metropolitan Counties in 1986). Indeed, these served as indicators of how thin the ice was that Labour Councils were treading on at the time. There are several 'signposts' that will serve to illustrate both the prospects for local government in the future and its role as part of a changing constitution.

We have seen how New Labour has embarked on a programme of constitutional change – devolution to Scotland and Wales, the Human Rights Act, Freedom of Information Act, the introduction of proportional representation for elections to the European Parliament – and local government has been conveniently inserted into this agenda as part of the drive towards modernisation (elected Mayors, Greater London Authority).

Constitutional reform was shared territory for New Labour and the Liberal Democrats in the 1990s, although disputes have arisen since (not least over local government) and this agenda was not necessarily shared by Labour Party members or local Councillors for that matter. However, New Labour's approach to constitutional reform has lacked co-ordination and consistency so it remains to be seen how the wider changes will affect local government and indeed how the changes in local government may, in turn, affect other areas of the constitution.

For instance, how will the tension between the mandates of an elected Mayor, their local MP and their GLA member be resolved if the officeholders are of different parties and wish to lobby Ministers and Civil Servants in Whitehall? It will, in all eventuality, probably fall down to the MP as the relevant elected member at that level and to whom the government is, in theory, directly accountable, thus reinforcing all prevailing notions of the 'sovereignty of Parliament'. There are no precedents for this and while it is an abstract example, other instances are imaginable where challenges to the sovereignty of Parliament may arise.

The relationship between local and central government in the twentieth century was very much a top-down affair, with the constitutional standpoint remaining that local government existed as long as Parliament wanted it to (this being reinforced by the Widdicombe Report in 1986). So far, any thinking on the constitution has not considered the effects of reform and how they may clash or indeed work against each other.

The much vaunted 'solution' to both local government's collective woes and the issue of elected legitimacy is the idea of the power of general competence, as discussed earlier. There are no signs that New Labour or the Conservatives would plan to introduce this (see Chapter Seven), very much the opposite in fact, although it does not receive the attention in the debate over the future of local democracy that it once did or still deserves.

The power of general competence, if in law, would solve the tensions between local and central government and act as a steady bedrock for its constitutional position, currently only found in a welter of legislation, much of which dates back to the feudal era. On another note, some thought should be given to how local government would fare under the Conservatives. Certainly the Tories have not exactly proved to be fearless champions of local democracy in the latter part of the twentieth century, although this was during an era when Labour was in a major position of strength in local government and a few sabres were rattled from below as well as above, not that this could ever excuse the severity of the government of the day's actions.

In any case, it is more than likely that the increasing number of hung Councils, restraint on the part of New Labour Councillors and the presence of Independent Councillors, will mean that local government under a Tory government will not lead to major confrontation between Councils and Whitehall in a way redolent of the 1980s.

In opposition, the Tories have opposed New Labour's reforms from the front-bench (although many Tory Councillors actually endorse the modernisation agenda) but have failed to successfully articulate an alternative agenda, with the phrase "more freedom for local Councils" being repeated over and over again without clarification as to what it means. Best Value has been derided but it is doubtful, in the same way as was the case with New Labour and CCT, that they would replace it with something else altogether and this also applies to elected Mayors, frequently derided yet hard to abolish because of their entrenched legitimacy by referendum. Indeed, in their struggle to redefine themselves and achieve electoral success once again, the Tories would be foolish not to reinvent themselves as the heirs to the Tory municipalist tradition as a means to rejuvenate the inner cities and move forward from their power bases in the County halls.

Cities of culture – why are some places better to live in than others?

This question, which has puzzled local politicians, academics and citizens, is also bound up in the recently floated concept of 'live-ability', promoted not just by local political leaders but Prime Minister Tony Blair himself. However, issues such as access to quality education and healthcare, community safety, cultural facilities and the local economy also take precedence in terms of making our communities better places to live.

Local government has the capacity to improve the lives of those it serves, but quite often for one reason or another finds itself incapable of doing so. When this happens, the usual stock response is to blame lack of resourcing from central government or the policies of a previous Council administration. In urban Britain all Councils are now single-tier all-purpose unitary authorities, so there is no-one to pass the buck to. While rural communities, themselves often no strangers to deprivation, have an entire central government department to look to, urban Britain finds governmental responsibility spread across departments of State. Furthermore, the Local Government Act 2000 places the duty on local Councils not only to look after the economic, social and environmental well-being of their communities, but also to exercise political leadership in the community.

The term 'Cities of Culture' is normally associated with rolling events such as the European Cities of Culture. But it now relates to the realisation that local authorities can influence cultural provision and access to culture in their localities. Urban design is increasing in importance in terms of local government's planning role, with participatory notions of local communities getting involved in their redesign becoming a recent trend – this once being the preserve of the 1960s Situationists (the brief Radical movement led by Guy Debord and his followers in late 1960s Paris) but having now made it onto the mainstream community regeneration agenda.

However, the cultural agenda and urban design are often seen as side-issues of little importance, especially when compared to the more economic and service-based issues that voters consider when they vote (or not, as is often the case in local elections). This is wilfully ignorant of the fact that access to cultural facilities is often a consideration when people decide to move to an area, although crime, transport and jobs still rank highly in most people's minds. Furthermore, cultural industries, both in the arts and service sectors, can make a significant contribution to the local economy, as well as creating a better perception of a locality as a place to live. This agenda encompasses two of local government's remaining 'quasi-judicial' functions – planning and licensing. The latter is a delicate balance between the interests of residents (who may not want a late night bar or club in their locality) and those who wish to participate in what is fast becoming a 24/7 society.

In the case of local government however, we have already seen that Councillors are either middle-aged or even elderly and therefore less likely to be sympathetic to late licensing applications. However, while some cities have led the way in cultural regeneration, this should not be mistaken for 'gentrification', which is guided by policy aspirations set with only part of the community in mind. In post-war Britain, the rise in car ownership saw the eventual demise of local public transport. However, the decline in manufacturing and the expansion of service industries has seen travel-to-work-areas increase in size, as well as a demonstrated need for better public transport to enable people to lead their lives according to the practices of the 24/7 society.

Cities that have led the way in mass transit provision include Newcastle, Manchester and to a lesser extent Sheffield, yet the notion of local intervention in this area seems to be an aspect of a bygone age. The 1985 Transport Act took away local government's remaining powers to actively provide in this area and only the six former Metropolitan Counties have Passenger Transport Authorities as a means of contributing a solution to our longstanding national problem in providing decent public transport.

All of these issues were considered at length by (Lord) Richard Rogers' Urban Task Force, which reported in 1999 and made a serious attempt at providing a blueprint for a renaissance in the fortunes of inner city Britain. In 2001 the Cantle report on community cohesion also examined the circumstances behind the deprivation in inner city areas and located the lack of local political leadership as a major contributing factor to the problem.

Even more recently, the Commons Select Committee on Environment, Transport and the Regions has argued in its report *The New Towns: their problems and future* that England's 'New Towns', created at various points in the twentieth century to foster notions of good design, planning and order, have decayed through poor infrastructure and cycles of deprivation and crime.

Therefore, it is not difficult to locate examples of public policy failure, but no one can rush to judge as to which level of government can be apportioned the blame. While a return to the Victorian era of municipal improvement cannot be viewed as befitting the problems of this century, although the idea of the 'public realm' harks back to that in part, local government needs ideals that it can work towards, and a cultural agenda that takes in all others is not a bad start by any means.

E-governance – downloaded democracy

Over the next few years no area of local government will be unaffected by the e-revolution.[94]

Geoff Mulgan

As recently as only a decade ago, few could have realised the extent to which the Internet would affect our lives in terms of making services more accessible and tailor-made for the consumer. The benefits of this for local government are many – library users can pay fines and reserve books over the Internet whereas local residents can pay housing benefit or parking fines through the same method. It also has other implications for Councils and their citizens – people can enquire about their child's school or university funding when it suits them rather than the usual 9-5 hours, apply for job, and progress chase their local Councillor on casework issues.

It has other interesting applications; for instance, would Internet-accessible party manifestos help to revive interest in local politics? There is only one way to find out.

As part of the growing interest in the concept of 'citizenship' under New Labour, e-democracy could lead to a more informed electorate, with spaces being set aside locally to debate local issues – indicative votes could be taken at Council meetings using a web cast, as happens in a number of local Councils at present. It certainly has implications for consultation exercises and could lead to increased interest and participation in these. Lewisham Council's Chief Executive Barry Quirk CBE has even suggested that e-government could make the local Councillor obsolete, as methods are developed to increase decision-making for local people over the Internet.

E-government is certainly not a threat to local democracy, it is an opportunity if anything, but some issues arise over access. For instance, those most likely to want to access Council services over the Internet will be the middle-class families in possession of a PC at home. This 'digital divide' represents an obstacle to rolling out Internet-led service provision on one hand but also provides a challenge in terms of ensuring more families (particularly the worse off) have access to the Internet, on the other.

The 'knowledge economy' advocated by champions of the e-government agenda such as Charles Leadbeater[95] will not take off if it is limited to only those who can afford to participate in it, although this is a well-worn out point. E-government does however represent an exciting challenge to local government and will have a major bearing on its future, although, in the same way that there were the curmudgeons who squealed with delight when the dotcom bubble burst, there are those who are not enthused by it amongst the legions of older Councillors.

Like other aspects of modernisation, the government has pushed the e-government agenda enthusiastically, although it does not appear to have filtered through to other public services such as the NHS in terms of being able to book an appointment with a doctor etc. Of particular relevance to local government, the government has made 2005 the date by which local authorities should have all services available electronically. In many areas this is realisable and desirable, such as the ability of voters to use the Internet to cast their vote in local elections. However, doubts have been raised regarding the likelihood of many Councils being able to achieve the government's target. In particular, the following issues have been outlined as possible obstacles:[96]

- 388 separate organisations
- Two or three tiers providing services in some areas
- A wide range of functions compared to central government
- Fewer ICT resources compared to central government.

However, with co-operation and readiness local Councils will prove capable of achieving this challenge, with many 'pathfinder' authorities already demonstrating this. Its champions have pointed out its capacity to revitalise local democracy but it is a technocratic agenda to many extents (this may explain the lack of enthusiasm amongst elected members) as it promotes the idea of Best Value even further, although it will require local political leadership to enable it to succeed.

This notwithstanding, the results of the voting reform pilots in the May 2002 local elections demonstrated that, where used, e-voting created more interest in local politics, and concerns regarding fraud and ease of use were nothing more than red herrings. As with anything else, it is a question of resources and digital equipment does not come cheaply, which in itself presents several social exclusion issues, bringing us back again to the 'digital divide'. The agenda is there and well known to all in local government; however, it is not seen as a major priority by many and the novelty may have already begun to wear off.

Current trends – the likelihood of further reform

Modernisation can come in a variety of forms – self-contained or continual immediately spring to mind. At first glance, it is a statement that suggests something is not up to scratch, in need of diagnosis and prescription. There is little to suggest that New Labour views modernisation in local government as a self-contained package, for once reform has taken place a new set of circumstances open up. However, it has applied this principle more consistently than in other areas of the constitution and the machinery of government.

The concept of political citizenship and the revival of civic virtue has gained currency under New Labour, initially under the bracket of democratic renewal, but now extolled as a fundamental tenet of New Labour thinking in itself. Citizenship, like the notion of 'community', has become a political football in many senses and it often drops off the lips of politicians without a second thought. Opportunities to extend citizenship and democracy exist within the realm of local government; after all it is the most immediate tier of government to most people. In particular, some regeneration initiatives have in-built mechanisms designed to foster an increased awareness of citizenship in communities where electoral turnout is often its lowest, such as the Get Set for Citizenship initiative under the New Cross Gate New Deal for Communities (turnout in 1998 in those wards hovered around the 21% mark, lower than the Borough average of 29.9%) which encourages community participation in local democratic structures.

Given its New Labour hue,[97] citizenship assumes duties of citizenship as well as democratic rights, hence the emphasis and reliance on Communitarian values in the local authority community safety agenda. However, the idea of citizenship at least assumes a modern, forward-looking local democracy, with open, transparent and accessible features, whereas 'subjecthood' is reliant on opaqueness, remote cliques of elderly white male Councillors and Mayors' chains.

The evolution of local democracy in Britain has brought with it differing views as to what form local government should take and how the local state should act on behalf of its citizens, with the 'gas and water socialism' of the early Fabians making a profound impact on communities in urban local authorities of the late nineteenth century, paving the way for local government's role as a provider in the welfare state of the post-war era. Throughout this period, the presence of Fabians in national government in the 1940s and 1960s-1970s saw the idea of local government as an instrument of state planning kept alive, with housing policies such as high-rise flats being advocated in Fabian pamphlets.

By the late twentieth century, however, local government's role had transmogrified into that of the 'enabling authority' in many Councils, with the local state's role being kept to a minimum. During the New Urban Left era in the 1980s, the Fabians as a national political organisation of the left were seemingly out of fashion. However, the ascendancy of New Labour in the 1990s saw the Fabians play an influential role in local government policy once more, with pamphlets such as Margaret Hodge's *Beyond the Town Hall*[98] bringing forward new thinking on local democracy. The Fabians advocated policies such as directly elected Mayors[99] that have been taken up by New Labour, whereas others like the abolition of the City of London Corporation[100] have not.

The case for electoral reform in local government was kept alight by torchbearers such as Stephen Twigg and Andrew Adonis in their Fabian pamphlet *The Cross We Bear*[101] and the modernisers of New Labour maintain it. The issue of proportional representation for local government was then ignited by the reform of the electoral system for the European Parliament and the adoption of proportional systems for Scotland, Wales and London. By this token, it is argued, local government should not be exempt from reform, after all there was a clear consensus in favour of proportional systems for the new democratic institutions (devolved assemblies and any reformed House of Lords). However, as with proportional representation for the House of Commons, the idea of electoral reform for local government has more than its fair share of opponents, not least among Councillors themselves.

As with national policy on all other democratic institutions, the Liberal Democrats advocate the use of the Single Transferable Vote (STV), whereas the Tories maintain a stance of opposition to reform, although there are some notable examples of dissention from this view amongst grassroots Tory Councillors, not least because it would open up representation to the Tories in the inner cities.[102] The arguments for or against electoral reform for local Councils could occupy an entire chapter, if not a book, but movement on this as an issue has stalled even under a Labour government.

In Scotland and Wales, the devolved governments have flirted with the issue, with the Scottish Parliament's Kerley Commission coming down in favour of the Single Transferable Vote system for Scottish Councils, which have long been Labour one-party states. Inside the M25 beltway, the issue is confined to the chattering classes and policy wonks, although the London Borough of Lewisham sought academic backing from experts Patrick Dunleavy and Helen Margetts and applied (unsuccessfully) to the DTLR to pilot the Additional Member System for its elections following a local 'Democracy Commission' recommending its adoption.

The momentum has been maintained academically by Steve Leach and Chris Game[103] and Patrick Dunleavy and Helen Margetts, who have maintained that the evolution of Cabinet government and the scrutiny activity in local authorities necessitates electoral reform and it is an issue to which the government at Westminster will need to return to as the changes in culture under the new Council regimes become more apparent.

The prospect of another round of Local Government Reorganisation in England to complete the task set by Michael Heseltine in the 1990s does not appear too likely under New Labour in this Parliament, although thinking on regional government has shown a tendency towards arguing for the abolition of the Counties. Proponents of the status quo are many; those with vested interests include Councils at County and district level, who would face either abolition or absorption under reorganisation and who were successful in deterring change only a decade ago.

However, it is patently obvious to any observer that the status quo cannot ensured, reorganisation into a unitary form of local government for England needs to happen, if only to facilitate regional government and demonstrate consistency with Scotland and Wales. But given the Tories' power bases in County halls across England and the interests of Labour district Councils being shored up by supporters on the Labour backbenches in Parliament, the obstacles remain for any government without the stubborn will to upset apple carts.

Reform seems most forthcoming in the 32 London Boroughs, alongside the new GLA and the plethora of Primary Care Groups and Trusts, represent the 'over governance' of the capital. Critics of the status quo maintain that a reduction in the number of London Boroughs (from 32 to 14 to shadow the GLA electoral divisions) is very much necessary, mainly because they do not command the allegiance of their residents who view their community (e.g. Kennington) as the focus for their civic identity, rather than their Borough (e.g. Lambeth).

Far from representing an assault on local democracy in the capital, this would see 'Super Boroughs' providing the strategic overview of local services, with Community Councils exercising both a representative role and a community focus for those services. The 1965 reorganisation removed Boroughs such as Finsbury and Camberwell from the map – the next round of reorganisation in London could see those areas return as Community Councils.

The evolution of local government in Britain, like any area of our unwritten constitution, has been slow and evolutionary. In Victorian Britain, local Councillors saw their role as being concerned with improving sanitation, developing public spaces and amenities (culminating in the New Towns movement) and sometimes to act as the guardians of public morals.

The recent emphasis on 'liveability' as a key service issue for both local and central government has seen this role revived somewhat. The last century saw an era of vast expansion in the activity of the local state in the fields of education and social services, as well as the provision of social housing, with tension between the centre and the localities on how these services could be best provided. Change and reform, of which the latter half of the last century saw plenty, have often been driven by the centre and resisted by local government itself.

Recent reforms such as the introduction of models of local political leadership will stand out in years to come. We will also see different forms of local government developing throughout the United Kingdom, with Scotland's devolved administration being able to take Scottish local government in a direction even further away from English Councils. The agenda of regionalism will certainly play a major part in the government's commitment to localism. As the closest tier of government to communities, local government had found itself in the driving seat on this agenda and through Local Strategic Partnerships; a more joined-up approach is in place to bring together both public agencies, such as the police, fire and health service, as well as business and the voluntary sector. Like schools and the NHS before them, local authorities have not proved to be immune from the government's fondness for monitoring performance through league tables, and citizens as consumers of local authority services will use government ratings when deciding where to live.

Failure to deliver in the public services and failure to promote social cohesion at the same time will render local government fertile territory for the anti-democratic extremist forces of the Far Right, who find Councils where seats can change hands by one vote to make for easier electoral breakthroughs than Parliament. Liveability may as well be a redundant concept on the 'sink estates' where these breakthroughs have taken place. As we have seen, local government is a key instrument of frontline delivery in the public services, yet the perceptions among the electorate do not befit this. In order to defeat both apathy and challenges from outside the political system, local government will have to grasp this improvement agenda and prove it is up to the job that it wasn't designed for in the first place.

Appendix I

Council of Europe – European Charter of Local Self-Government
Preamble
The member States of the Council of Europe, signatory hereto,

* Considering that the aim of the Council of Europe is to achieve a greater unity between its members for the purpose of safeguarding and realising the ideals and principles which are their common heritage;
* Considering that one of the methods by which this aim is to be achieved is through agreements in the administrative field;
* Considering that the local authorities are one of the main foundations of any democratic regime;
* Considering that the right of citizens to participate in the conduct of public affairs is one of the democratic principles that are shared by all member States of the Council of Europe;
* Considering that it is at local level that this right can be most directly exercised;
* Convinced that the existence of local authorities with real responsibilities can provide an administration which is both effective and close to the citizen;
* Aware that the safeguarding and reinforcement of local self-government in the different European countries is an important contribution to the construction of a Europe based on the principles of democracy and the decentralisation of power;
* Asserting that this entails the existence of local authorities endowed with democratically constituted decision-making bodies and possessing a wide degree of autonomy with regard to their responsibilities, the ways and means by which those responsibilities are exercised and the resources required for their fulfilment,

Have agreed as follows:

Article 1
The Parties undertake to consider themselves bound by the following articles in the manner and to the extent prescribed in Article 12 of this Charter.

Part I
Article 2 – Constitutional and legal foundation for local self-government
The principle of local self-government shall be recognised in domestic legislation, and where practicable in the constitution.

Article 3 – Concept of local self-government
1   Local self-government denotes the right and the ability of local authorities, within the

limits of the law, to regulate and manage a substantial share of public affairs under their own responsibility and in the interests of the local population.

2   This right shall be exercised by councils or assemblies composed of members freely elected by secret ballot on the basis of direct, equal, universal suffrage, and which may possess executive organs responsible to them. This provision shall in no way affect recourse to assemblies of citizens, referendums or any other form of direct citizen participation where it is permitted by statute.

Article 4 – Scope of local self-government

1   The basic powers and responsibilities of local authorities shall be prescribed by the constitution or by statute. However, this provision shall not prevent the attribution to local authorities of powers and responsibilities for specific purposes in accordance with the law.

2   Local authorities shall, within the limits of the law, have full discretion to exercise their initiative with regard to any matter, which is not excluded from their competence nor assigned to any other authority.

3   Public responsibilities shall generally be exercised, in preference, by those authorities that are closest to the citizen. Allocation of responsibility to another authority should weigh up the extent and nature of the task and requirements of efficiency and economy.

4   Powers given to local authorities shall normally be full and exclusive. They may not be undermined or limited by another, central or regional, authority except as provided for by the law.

5   Where powers are delegated to them by a central or regional authority, local authorities shall, insofar as possible, be allowed discretion in adapting their exercise to local conditions.

6   Local authorities shall be consulted, insofar as possible, in due time and in an appropriate way in the planning and decision-making processes for all matters which concern them directly.

Article 5 – Protection of local authority boundaries

Changes in local authority boundaries shall not be made without prior consultation of the local communities concerned, possibly by means of a referendum where this is permitted by statute.

Article 6 – Appropriate administrative structures and resources for the tasks of local authorities

1   Without prejudice to more general statutory provisions, local authorities shall be able to determine their own internal administrative structures in order to adapt them to local needs and ensure effective management.

2   The conditions of service of local government employees shall be such as to permit the recruitment of high-quality staff on the basis of merit and competence; to this end adequate training opportunities, remuneration and career prospects shall be provided.

Article 7 – Conditions under which responsibilities at local level are exercised

1   The conditions of office of local elected representatives shall provide for free exercise of

their functions.

2 They shall allow for appropriate financial compensation for expenses incurred in the exercise of the office in question as well as, where appropriate, compensation for loss of earnings or remuneration for work done and corresponding social welfare protection.

3 Any functions and activities, which are deemed incompatible with the holding of local elective office, shall be determined by statute or fundamental legal principles.

Article 8 – Administrative supervision of local authorities' activities

1 Any administrative supervision of local authorities may only be exercised according to such procedures and in such cases as are provided for by the constitution or by statute.

2 Any administrative supervision of the activities of the local authorities shall normally aim only at ensuring compliance with the law and with constitutional principles. Administrative supervision may however be exercised with regard to expediency by higher-level authorities in respect of tasks the execution of which is delegated to local authorities.

3 Administrative supervision of local authorities shall be exercised in such a way as to ensure that the intervention of the controlling authority is kept in proportion to the importance of the interests that it is intended to protect.

Article 9 – Financial resources of local authorities

1 Local authorities shall be entitled, within national economic policy, to adequate financial resources of their own, of which they may dispose freely within the framework of their powers.

2 Local authorities' financial resources shall be commensurate with the responsibilities provided for by the constitution and the law.

3 Part at least of the financial resources of local authorities shall derive from local taxes and charges of which, within the limits of statute, they have the power to determine the rate.

4 The financial systems on which resources available to local authorities are based shall be of a sufficiently diversified and buoyant nature to enable them to keep pace as far as practically possible with the real evolution of the cost of carrying out their tasks.

5 The protection of financially weaker local authorities calls for the institution of financial equalisation procedures or equivalent measures which are designed to correct the effects of the unequal distribution of potential sources of finance and of the financial burden they must support. Such procedures or measures shall not diminish the discretion local authorities may exercise within their own sphere of responsibility.

6 Local authorities shall be consulted, in an appropriate manner, on the way in which redistributed resources are to be allocated to them.

7 As far as possible, grants to local authorities shall not be earmarked for the financing of specific projects. The provision of grants shall not remove the basic freedom of local authorities to exercise policy discretion within their own jurisdiction.

8 For the purpose of borrowing for capital investment, local authorities shall have access to the national capital market within the limits of the law.

<u>Article 10 – Local authorities' right to associate</u>
1   Local authorities shall be entitled, in exercising their powers, to co-operate and, within the framework of the law, to form consortia with other local authorities in order to carry out tasks of common interest.
2   The entitlement of local authorities to belong to an association for the protection and promotion of their common interests and to belong to an international association of local authorities shall be recognised in each State.
3   Local authorities shall be entitled, under such conditions as may be provided for by the law, to co-operate with their counterparts in other States.

<u>Article 11 – Legal protection of local self-government</u>
Local authorities shall have the right of recourse to a judicial remedy in order to secure free exercise of their powers and respect for such principles of local self-government as are enshrined in the constitution or domestic legislation.

Part II – Miscellaneous provisions
<u>Article 12 – Undertakings</u>
1   Each Party undertakes to consider itself bound by at least twenty paragraphs of Part I of the Charter, at least ten of which shall be selected from among the following paragraphs:
  • Article 2,
  • Article 3, paragraphs 1 and 2,
  • Article 4, paragraphs 1, 2 and 4,
  • Article 5,
  • Article 7, paragraph 1,
  • Article 8, paragraph 2,
  • Article 9, paragraphs 1, 2 and 3,
  • Article 10, paragraph 1,
  • Article 11.
2   Each Contracting State, when depositing its instrument of ratification, acceptance or approval, shall notify to the Secretary General of the Council of Europe of the paragraphs selected in accordance with the provisions of paragraph 1 of this article.
3   Any Party may, at any later time, notify the Secretary General that it considers itself bound by any paragraphs of this Charter, which it has not already accepted under the terms of paragraph 1 of this article. Such undertakings subsequently given shall be deemed to be an integral part of the ratification, acceptance or approval of the Party so notifying, and shall have the same effect as from the first day of the month following the expiration of a period of three months after the date of the receipt of the notification by the Secretary General.

<u>Article 13 – Authorities to which the Charter applies</u>
The principles of local self-government contained in the present Charter apply to all the categories of local authorities existing within the territory of the Party. However, each Party may, when depositing its instrument of ratification, acceptance or approval, specify the categories

of local or regional authorities to which it intends to confine the scope of the Charter or which it intends to exclude from its scope. It may also include further categories of local or regional authorities within the scope of the Charter by subsequent notification to the Secretary General of the Council of Europe.

Article 14 – Provision of information
Each Party shall forward to the Secretary General of the Council of Europe all relevant information concerning legislative provisions and other measures taken by it for the purposes of complying with the terms of this Charter.

Part III
Article 15 – Signature, ratification and entry into force
1   This Charter shall be open for signature by the member States of the Council of Europe. It is subject to ratification, acceptance or approval. Instruments of ratification, acceptance or approval shall be deposited with the Secretary General of the Council of Europe.
2   This Charter shall enter into force on the first day of the month following the expiration of a period of three months after the date on which four member States of the Council of Europe have expressed their consent to be bound by the Charter in accordance with the provisions of the preceding paragraph.
3   In respect of any member State that subsequently expresses its consent to be bound by it, the Charter shall enter into force on the first day of the month following the expiration of a period of three months after the date of the deposit of the instrument of ratification, acceptance or approval.

Article 16 – Territorial clause
1   Any State may, at the time of signature or when depositing its instrument of ratification, acceptance, approval or accession, specify the territory or territories to which this Charter shall apply.
2   Any State may at any later date, by a declaration addressed to the Secretary General of the Council of Europe, extend the application of this Charter to any other territory specified in the declaration. In respect of such territory the Charter shall enter into force on the first day of the month following the expiration of a period of three months after the date of receipt of such declaration by the Secretary General.
3   Any declaration made under the two preceding paragraphs may, in respect of any territory specified in such declaration, be withdrawn by a notification addressed to the Secretary General. The withdrawal shall become effective on the first day of the month following the expiration of a period of six months after the date of receipt of such notification by the Secretary General.

Article 17 – Denunciation
1   Any Party may denounce this Charter at any time after the expiration of a period of five years from the date on which the Charter entered into force for it. Six months' notice shall be given to the Secretary General of the Council of Europe. Such denunciation shall

not affect the validity of the Charter in respect of the other Parties provided that at all times there are not less than four such Parties.

2 Any Party may, in accordance with the provisions set out in the preceding paragraph, denounce any paragraph of Part I of the Charter accepted by it provided that the Party remains bound by the number and type of paragraphs stipulated in Article 12, paragraph 1. Any Party that, upon denouncing a paragraph, no longer meets the requirements of Article 12, paragraph 1, shall be considered as also having denounced the Charter itself.

Article 18 – Notifications

The Secretary General of the Council of Europe shall notify the member States of the Council of Europe of:

    a   any signature;

    b   the deposit of any instrument of ratification, acceptance or approval;

    c   any date of entry into force of this Charter in accordance with Article 15;

    d   any notification received in application of the provisions of Article 12, paragraphs 2 and 3;

    e   any notification received in application of the provisions of Article 13;

    f   any other act, notification or communication relating to this Charter.

In witness whereof the undersigned, being duly authorised thereto, have signed this Charter.

Done at Strasbourg, this 15th day of October 1985, in English and French, both texts being equally authentic, in a single copy that shall be deposited in the archives of the Council of Europe. The Secretary General of the Council of Europe shall transmit certified copies to each member State of the Council of Europe.

Appendix II

Organisations responsible for local government
Local government in England is now handled by the Office of the Deputy Prime Minister. However, in June 2001 the newly created Department for Transport, Local Government and the Regions (DTLR) assumed responsibility for all areas of local government operations, including some of those previously held by the Home Office. Previously this was held by the Department of Environment, Transport and the Regions (which replaced the Department of the Environment in 1997, which was itself created from a merger of the Ministry of Housing and the Ministry of Local Government in 1970). A Minister for Local Government provides the ministerial lead on local government matters within central government and the Cabinet brief is currently held by the Deputy Prime Minister. Separate arrangements exist for Scotland and Wales.

Office of the Deputy Prime Minister
Eland House
Bressenden Place
London SW1E 5DU
Tel 020 7944 3000
Website: www.odpm.gov.uk and www.info4local.gov.uk
e-mail: See main website for individual e mail addresses

Commission for Local Administration in England (Ombudsmen)
21 Queen Anne's Gate
London SW1H 9BU
Tel: 020 7915 3210
Fax: 020 7233 0396
Website:: www.lgo.org.uk

The Local Government Ombudsmen exist to "investigate complaints of injustice arising from maladministration by local authorities".

Audit Commission
1 Vincent Square
London SW1P 2PN
Tel: 020 7828 1212
Fax: 020 7976 6187
Website: www.audit-commission.gov.uk
e-mail: enquiries@audit-commission.gov.uk

The Audit Commission is "an independent body responsible for ensuring that public money is used economically, efficiently and effectively". The Audit Commission carries out national research on public sector delivery performance. It is also responsible for appointing external auditors to audit the financial statements and to carry out reviews of governance arrangements and performance in all local authorities.

Local Government Commission for England
Dolphyn Court
10-11 Great Turnstile
London WC1V 7JU
Tel: 020 7430 8400
Fax: 020 7404 6140
Website: www.lgce.gov.uk
e-mail: reviews@lgce.gov.uk

The Local Government Commission for England was set up in 1992 to review the boundaries and structures of English local authorities on a rolling basis. It presided over the Local Government Reorganisation in the mid 1990s, which aimed to construct a unitary form of local government for England.

Standards Board for England
St. Christopher House
98–104 Southwark Street
London SE1 OTE
Tel: 020 7921 1800
Fax: 020 7921 1801
Website: www.standardsboard.co.uk
e-mail: enquiries@standardsboard.co.uk

The Standards Board for England was set up in 2001 to "ensure that the highest standards of ethical conduct are maintained across local government and to deal with complaints of misconduct against individual members".

Organisations representing and supporting local government
Several umbrella groups exist to either support or represent the collective interests of local authorities.

Local Government Association
Local Government House
Smith Square
London SW1P 3HZ
Tel: 020 7664 3000
Fax: 020 7664 3030

Website: www.lga.gov.uk
e-mail: info@lga.gov.uk

The LGA, an umbrella group for the collective interests of local authorities, was formed in 1996 following the merger of the Association of District Councils, the Association of County Councils and the Association of Metropolitan Authorities. Its mission is to "promote better local government".

National Association of Local Councils
109 Great Russell Street
London WC1B 3LD
Tel: 020 7637 1865
Fax: 020 7436 7451
Website: www.nalc.gov.uk
e-mail: nalc@nalc.gov.uk

The National Association of Local Councils was established in 1947 to represent the interests of English Town and Parish Councils and Welsh Community Councils. It is committed to "making this primary level of local government more effective, more democratic and better able to take a leadership role in local communities".

County Councils Network
Local Government House
Smith Square
London SW1P 3HZ
Tel: 020 7664 3005
Website: www.lga.gov.uk/ccn/
e-mail: sue.hood@lga.gov.uk

The County Councils Network is a Special Interest Group within the Local Government Association (LGA), with all 35 English Shire Counties in membership. Together these authorities represent 47% of the population of England and provide services across 84% of its land area.

Welsh Local Government Association
Local Government House
Drake Walk
Cardiff CF10 4LG
Tel: 029 204 68600
Fax: 029 204 68601
Website: www.wlga.gov.uk
e-mail: enquiries@wlga.gov.uk

The WLGA is the Welsh arm of the Local Government Association, representing local authorities in Wales.

Confederation of Scottish Local Authorities (COSLA)
Rosebery House
9 Haymarket Terrace
Rosebery House
Edinburgh EH12 5XZ
Tel: 0131 474 9200
Fax: 0131 474 9292
Website: www.cosla.gov.uk
e-mail: enquiries@cosla.gov.uk

COSLA is the representative voice of Scotland's unitary local authorities and "has a responsibility to develop, encourage and promote best practice in partnership with its member Councils".

Local Government International Bureau
Local Government House
Smith Square
London SW1P 3HZ
Tel: 020 7664 3100
Fax: 020 7664 3128
Website: www.lgib.gov.uk
e-mail: enquiries@lgib.gov.uk

The LGIB represents the interests of local government internationally and in Europe. It provides services to local authorities through research and partnerships.

Commonwealth Local Government Forum
59½ Southwark Street
London SE1 0AL
Tel: 020 7934 9690
Fax: 020 7934 9699
Website: www.clgf.org.uk
e-mail: info@clgf.org.uk

The Commonwealth Local Government Forum (CLGF) was founded in 1995, as a focus for action on local democracy in the Commonwealth and was endorsed by Commonwealth Heads of Government at their meeting in New Zealand that year. As the local government arm of the Commonwealth, CLGF has been actively involved in encouraging and developing local elections and systems, election monitoring, and capacity building support for Councillors and Councils.

Improvement and Development Agency (IDeA)
Layden House
76-86 Turnmill Street

Politico's guide to local government

London EC1M 5LG
Tel: 020 7296 6693
Fax: 020 7296 6666
Website: www.idea.gov.uk
e-mail: info@idea.gov.uk
Established by and for local government, the Improvement and Development Agency (IDeA) draws expertise from local authorities, the business world, professional service firms, and not for profit organisations as well as other parts of the public sector.

Inter Authorities Group
PO Box 19436
London E4 6FH
Tel: 07970 251854
Website: www.iag.org.uk
e-mail: jane.weaver@iag.org.uk

Founded in 1992, the Inter Authorities Group is an independent, non-political, non-profit making association of over 100 UK local authorities and other public bodies dedicated to sharing best practice and the benchmarking of public services.

Employers' Organisation
Layden House
76-86 Turnmill Street
London
EC1M 5LG
Tel: 020 7296 6600
Fax: 020 7296 6666
Website: www.lg-employers.gov.uk

The Employers' Organisation for local government (EO) was founded in April 1999, to support local authorities in their human resources role.

Local Government Information
Unit 22 Upper Woburn Place
London
WC1H 0TB
Tel: 020 7554 2800
Fax: 020 7554 2801
Website: www.lgiu.gov.uk
e-mail: info@lgiu.org.uk

The LGIU is an independent research and information organisation supported by over 150 Councils and the local government trade unions.

INLOGOV
School of Public Policy
University of Birmingham
Edgbaston
Birmingham B15 2TT
Tel: 0121 414 3872/5008
Fax: 0121 414 4954/4989
Website: spp3.bham.ac.uk/dlgs/
e-mail: S.K.Purba@bham.ac.uk

INLOGOV (the University of Birmingham's Institute of Local Government) aims to be "the leading Institute for research in local governance, public policy and management".

Association of London Government
59½ Southwark Street
London SE1 0AL
Tel: 020 7934 9999
Website: www.alg.gov.uk
e-mail: info@alg.gov.uk

The ALG was launched in April 2000 to speak up for local government in the capital. This includes the 32 Boroughs, the City of London Corporation, the Metropolitan Police Authority and the London Fire and Emergency Planning Authority.

Association for Public Service Excellence
4th Floor, Olympic House
Whitworth Street West
Manchester M1 5WG
Tel: 0161 236 8433
Fax: 0161 236 6479
Website: www.apse.org.uk
e-mail: enquiries@apse.org.uk

APSE was formed in the early 1980s in response to the 1980 Planning and Land Act and was expanded to deal with the extension of CCT in the 1988 Local Government Act and again when white-collar services were subjected to CCT. With the demise of CCT, APSE has now refocused itself around Best Value issues.

New Local Government Network
2nd Floor
42 Southwark Street
London SE1 1UN

Politico's guide to local government

Tel: 020 7357 0051
Fax: 020 7357 0404
Website: www.nlgn.org.uk
e-mail: network@nlgn.org.uk

The aim of the New Local Government Network is to "promote fresh and innovative thinking about the modernisation agenda for local government" in order to "transform public services, revitalise local political leadership and empower local communities".

Centre for Public Services
Sidney Street
Sheffield S1 4RG.
Tel: 0114 272 6683
Fax: 0114 272 7066
Website:: www.centre.public.org.uk
e-mail: ctr.public.serv@mcr1.poptel.org.uk

The Centre for Public Services is an independent, non-profit organisation. It is committed to the provision of good quality public services by democratically accountable public bodies implementing best practice management, employment and equal opportunities policies. It has a strong emphasis on local government issues.

Local Government Trade Press
Local government is supported by a variety of independent publications covering a wide range of political issues affecting local democracy.

Local Government Chronicle
Greater London House
Hampstead Road
London NW1 7EJ
020 76347 1818
(weekly)

Municipal Journal
32 Vauxhall Bridge Road
London SW1V 2SS
020 7973 6400
(weekly)

Local Government News
Hereford House
Bridle Path
Croydon CR9 4NL

020 8680 4200
(monthly)

Local Government First
Local Government House
Smith Square
London SW1P 3HZ
020 7664 3000
(monthly)

Careers in Local Government
The staple reading for anyone seeking a career in local government is the Jobs section in Wednesday's the *Guardian* (also available online at www.guardian.co.uk). In addition, many local authorities and agencies carry their existing vacancies on their own websites (go to www.ukonline.gov.uk/quickfind/local for an index of all British local authorities) or at www.opportunities.co.uk. Good sites can also be found at www.lgjobs.com and www.jobsgopublic.com.

Appendix III

Key Local Government Legislation and its effects

1834 Poor Law Amendment Act
To remove the responsibility for the poor from Parishes and transfer this to the Boards of Guardians

1835 Municipal Corporations Act
To allow for Town Councillors to be directly elected from the common ratepayers' franchise in the Boroughs and introduce new financial probity and accountability regimes

1847 Fire Brigades Act
To enable local authorities to provide local fire brigades

1848 Artisans and Labourers' Dwellings Act
To enable local authorities to provide some social housing

1848 Public Health Act
To empower local authorities to remove nuisance and prevent disease

1850 Small Tenements Rating Act
To enable the collection of the rates from the poor (and therefore widen the franchise)

1855 Metropolis Local Management Act
To create 99 parish areas for London and a Metropolitan Board of Works to supervise sanitation for the capital

1858 Local Government Act
To provide for the removal of nuisances and prevention of disease

1862 Highways Act
To establish Highways Boards, mainly in rural areas

1870 Education Act
To establish elected School Boards to administer free state education

1875 Public Health Act
To increase the powers of local authorities to improve health and sanitation

1882 Municipal Corporations Act
To state the role of the Mayor in a Borough

1888 Local Government Act
To create elected County Councils in Shire areas and County Boroughs in urban areas

1890 Housing Act
To provide further authority to provide social housing as a public health responsibility

1890 Lunacy Act
To require local authorities to detain and treat the mentally ill

1894 Local Government Act
To create Urban District and Rural District Councils from the various boards and Parishes

1902 Education Act
To create Local Education Authorities amongst the Counties and larger Boroughs in order to replace School Boards

1909 Housing, Town Planning & etc Act
To empower local authorities to introduce town planning schemes

1913 Mental Deficiency Act
To extend the powers of local authorities to detain non-lunatics

1919 Housing and Town Planning Act
To enable local authorities to provide comprehensive social housing

1925 Rating and Valuation Act
To enable local authorities to possess quasi-judicial powers to set and rule on rateable values

1929 Local Government Act
To abolish the Boards of Guardians for the Poor and reduce the number of District Councils

1930 Poor Law Act
To establish a specific Council committee for poor relief

1930 Mental Treatment Act
To require local authorities to accommodate the mentally ill

1931 Local Government Act
To set the terms and conditions for the employment of County Clerks

1932 Town and Country Planning Act
To extend the powers of town planning to County Councils

1933 Local Government Act
To enable several local authorities to establish joint committees with remits of local instance

1936 Public Health Act
To increase the duties of local authorities in respect of public health and sanitation

1936 Housing Act
To grant local authorities the power to oblige private landlords to ensure housing is fit for human habitation

1938 Fire Brigades Act
To require local authorities to provide public fire protection

1944 Education Act
To require all LEAs to provide teachers and schools for all children of up to 15 years old

1946 National Health Service Act
To transfer local authority hospitals to Regional Health Boards

1948 National Assistance Act
To abolish the Poor Law in its entirety

1948 Children Act
To oblige local authorities to take care of deprived children

1963 London Government Act
To replace the London County Council with a Greater London Council

1968 Transport Act
To establish Passenger Transport Authorities in several metropolitan areas

1970 Local Authorities Social Services Act
To create individual social services departments within local authorities

1972 Local Government Act
To implement the recommendations of the Redcliffe-Maud Report and create a two-tier system of Counties and Districts

1973 National Health Service Act
To transfer remaining local authority responsibilities for health to Area Health Authorities

1974 Local Government Act
To create the office of the Local Government Commissioners (Ombudsmen)

1980 Local Government Planning and Land Act
To introduce the 'right to buy' for Council housing, competitive tendering, Urban Development Corporations and block grants

1982 Local Government Finance Act
To establish the Audit Commission and abolish supplementary rates

1984 Rates Act
To introduce rate-capping

1985 Local Government Act
To abolish the Greater London Council and the six Metropolitan County Councils

1985 Local Government (Access to Information) Act
To allow for public access to Council committee meetings and committee papers

1988 Local Government Act
To make competitive tendering compulsory

1988 Local Government Finance Act
To introduce the Community Charge ('Poll Tax') to England and Wales and national business rates

1988 Education Reform Act
To introduce local financial management in schools and the right of schools to opt out of local authority control (Grant Maintained Schools) and remove polytechnics from LEA control

1989 Local Government and Housing Act
To introduce political restriction for local government officers (the 'Widdicombe Ban') and the requirement to allocate seats on committees according to party strength, and to ban Council rent subsidies

1990 Environmental Protection Act
To empower local authorities to regulate the local environment

1990 National Health Service and Community Care Act
To remove local authority representation on local health authorities

1992 Local Government Act
To create the Local Government Commission to review structures in order to move towards a unitary structure of local government

1992 Food Act
To empower local authorities to inspect premises used to prepare and sell food

1992 Further and Higher Education Act
To remove local FE and sixth form colleges from LEA control

1994 Local Government (Wales) Act
To reform Welsh local government into 22 unitary authorities

1994 Local Government (Scotland) Act
To reform Scottish local government into 32 unitary local authorities

1994 Police and Magistrates' Courts Act
To reduce local councils' representation on local Police Authorities by half

1997 Local Government (Contracts) Act
To confirm the power of councils to arrange for the private provision of services

1997 Local Government and Rating Act
To increase the powers of Parish Councils and remove rates exemption from Crown property

1998 School Standards and Framework Act
To establish Education Action Zones, abolish Grant Maintained Schools, allow local ballots on the future of local selective schools and allow Ministers to take over failing LEAs and individual schools

1998 Government of Scotland Act
To establish the devolved Scottish Parliament (who now oversee Scottish local government)

1998 Government of Wales Act
To transfer the Secretary of State for Wales' powers concerning Welsh local authorities to the Welsh Assembly

1998 Regional Development Agencies Act
To establish regional bodies for strategic and economic planning

1998 Public Interest Disclosure Act
To protect whistleblowers against loss of employment from reporting corruption

1998 Human Rights Act
To ratify the European Convention on Human Rights into UK law (affects all public bodies)

1998 Crime and Disorder Act
To establish a statutory role for local authorities in community safety

1999 Local Government Act
To abolish general capping and introduce Best Value regime

1999 Greater London Authority Act
To establish the Greater London Authority, a directly elected Mayor for London and a 25-member Assembly elected under proportional representation

2000 Freedom of Information Act
To provide a statutory right of access to information and a duty for local authorities to publish information

2000 Local Government Act
To require local authorities to promote the economic, social and environmental well-being of their areas; the duty to publish community strategies; new standards arrangements; abolish the surcharge and the introduction of new executive management arrangements, including directly elected Mayors

2000 Representation of the People Act
To introduce a rolling electoral register

2000 Learning and Skills Act
To establish local Learning and Skills Councils with local authority representation, abolish local Training and Enterprise Councils, and extend OFSTED inspection to FE colleges and sixth forms

Appendix IV

Boundaries and Responsibilities

Notes of types of local authority

There are a total of 410 local authorities in England and Wales. In Scotland, Wales and urban areas of England single-tier unitary authorities provide all local services, whereas the remainder of England is served by a two-tier system split between District and County Councils.

There are 34 County Councils in England and these cover a further 238 smaller District Councils (sometimes known as Boroughs). In addition to these there are 22 Welsh unitary authorities and 116 Unitary Councils covering English urban areas. These can be broken down into:

English Shires (47)	Unitary Authorities
Greater Manchester (10)	Metropolitan Authorities
Merseyside (5)	Metropolitan Authorities
South Yorkshire (4)	Metropolitan Authorities
Tyne and Wear (5)	Metropolitan Authorities
West Midlands (7)	Metropolitan Authorities
West Yorkshire (5)	Metropolitan Authorities
Greater London (33)	London Boroughs

There are also 10 000 Parish/Town Councils in England (Community Councils in Wales) and these fulfil a more localised role where they exist, such as allotments and street lighting. A small number of these have the ceremonial title of City, hailing from when they were Boroughs in their own right before absorption into larger units under reorganisation. These are:

- Chichester
- Ely
- Hereford
- Lichfield
- Ripon
- Truro
- Wells

Under the two-tier system, the lower tier is recognised as Districts, although some of these may have status as Boroughs through old Royal Charters conferred upon them. This also applies to Cities, although a number of Boroughs have been converted into Cities in recent times through the conferral of Royal Charters upon them. All local authorities have Chairmen or Mayors as ceremonial/civic figureheads; in some larger urban areas they may have Lord Mayors. Where an authority is called a District Council it will have a Chairman and where the authority is a Borough or City Council it will have a Mayor or Lord Mayor.

Bibliography

Hugh Atkinson and Stuart Wilks-Heeg, *Local Government from Thatcher to Blair*, 2000

Walter Bagehot, *The English Constitution* (2nd ed), 1872

David Blunkett and Geoff Green, *Democracy in Crisis*, 1987

David Blunkett, *Politics and Progress*, 2001

David Butler and Gareth Butler, *British Political Facts 1900-94*, 1995

Tony Byrne, *Local Government in Britain* (7th ed), 2000

David Coates and Peter Lawler (eds), *New Labour in power*, 2000

Cynthia Cockburn, *The Local State: management of Cities and people*, 1977

G.D.H. Cole, *History of the Labour Party*, 1948

Anthony Crosland, *The Future of Socialism*, 1956

Mark D'Arcy and Rory MacLean, *Nightmare!*, 2000

Patrick Dunleavy, *Urban Political Analysis*, 1980

Howard Elcock, *Local Government: Policy and Management in Local Authorities* (3rd ed), 1994

Ron Fenney, *Essential Local Government* (10th ed), 2002

John Gyford, *The politics of Local Socialism*, 1985

Lord Hailsham, *The Dilemma of Democracy*, 1978

Peter Hennessy, *Never Again*, 1992

P.W.Jackson, *Local Government*, 1970

Peter Jenkins, *Mrs Thatcher's Revolution: The Ending of The Socialist Era*, 1987

Sir Ivor Jennings, *Principles of Local Government Law*, 1965

W.I.Jennings, H.Laski and W.A.Robson, *A century of municipal progress: The last hundred years*, 1935

George Jones and John Stewart, *The Case for Local Government*, 1985

John Kingdom, *Local Government and Politics in Britain*, 1991

Labour Party, *Renewing democracy, rebuilding communities*, 1995

Stuart Lansley, Sue Goss and Christian Wolmar, *Councils in Conflict: The Rise and Fall of the Municipal Left*, 1989

Harold J.Laski, *A Grammar of Politics*, 1938

Neal Lawson and Neil Sherlock (eds) *The Progressive Century*, 2000

Steve Leach and David Wilson, *Local Political Leadership*, 2000

Charles Leadbeater, *Living on Thin Air*, 2000

M.Loughlan, M.D. Gelfand and K.Young (eds), *Half a Century of Municipal Decline 1935-1985*, 1985

Brian Lucas and P.G.Richards, *A History of Local Government in the Twentieth Century*, 1978

Leo McKinistry, *Fit to Govern?*, 1996

Ralph Miliband, *Capitalist Democracy in Britain*, 1982

J.L.Motley, *The Rise of the Dutch Republic*, 1853

Politico's guide to local government

John Morrison, *Reforming Britain*, 2001

Janet Newman, *Modernising Governance*, 2001

Nirmala Rao, *The Making and Un-making of Local Self-government*, 1994

Nirmala Rao, *Reviving Local Democracy*, 2000

J.Redlich and F.W.Hirst, *Local Government in England*, 1903

John Stewart and Gerry Stoker (eds), *Local Government in the 1990s*, 1995

Gerry Stoker, *The Politics of Local Government*, 1991

Gerry Stoker (ed), *The New Politics of British Local Governance*, 2000

Peter Taafe and Tony Mulhearn, *Liverpool – A City That Dared To Fight*, 1988

Tony Travers, *The Politics of Local Government Finance*, 1989

David Wilson and Chris Game, *Local Government in the United Kingdom* (2nd ed), 1998

Ken Young and Nirmala Rao, *Local Government Since 1945*, 1997

Endnotes

1 Harold J.Laski, *A Grammar of Politics*, 1938
2 Ibid.
3 Walter Bagehot, *The English Constitution* (2nd ed), 1872
4 Lord Levene, former Lord Mayor of London, in the *Wall Street Journal*, March 1996
5 Terms of reference for the 1833 Royal Commission to Inquire into the Municipal Corporations
6 Sidney Webb, *Socialism in England*, 1890
7 John Stuart Mill, *Considerations on Representative Government*, 1861
8 G.D.H. Cole, *History of the Labour Party*, 1948
9 John Gyford, *The politics of Local Socialism*, 1985
10 J.Redlich and F.W.Hirst, *Local Government in England*, 1903
11 Anthony Crosland, *The Future of Socialism*, 1956
12 In Peter Hennessy, *Never Again*, 1992
13 Evelyn Sharp, 'The future of local government', in *Public Administration*, Vol.40
14 Tony Byrne, *Local Government in Britain* (7th ed), 2000
15 Ron Fenney, *Essential Local Government* (10th ed), 2002
16 In David Butler and Gareth Butler, *British Political Facts 1900-94*, 1995
17 Ralph Miliband, *Capitalist Democracy in Britain*, 1982
18 David Blunkett and Geoff Green, *Building from the Bottom: The Sheffield Experience* (Fabian Society Pamphlet), 1983
19 David Blunkett and Geoff Green, *Democracy in Crisis*, 1987
20 Stuart Lansley, Sue Goss and Christian Wolmar, *Councils in Conflict: The Rise and Fall of the Municipal Left*, 1989
21 Gerry Stoker, *The Politics of Local Government*, 1991
22 Peter Taafe and Tony Mulhearn, *Liverpool – A City That Dared To Fight*, 1988
23 Peter Jenkins, *Mrs Thatcher's Revolution: The Ending of The Socialist Era*, 1987
24 Local Government Act 1988
25 Leo McKinistry, *Fit to Govern?*, 1996
26 Lord Hailsham, *The Dilemma of Democracy*, 1978
27 Sir Ivor Jennings, *Principles of Local Government Law*, 1965
28 John Kingdom, *Local Government and Politics in Britain*, 1991
29 Ibid.
30 Report of the Widdicombe Committee on The Conduct of Local Authority Business, 1986
31 Laski, op cit.
32 David Wilson and Chris Game, *Local Government in the United Kingdom* (2nd ed), 1998
33 Ibid.

34   Andrew Stevens, Paul Simpson et al, Redesigning Local Democracy (New Politics Network), 2002

35   Tony Travers, 'Finance', in John Stewart and Gerry Stoker (eds), Local Government in the 1990s, 1995

36   Tony Byrne, 2000

37   DTLR, Strong Local Leadership – Quality Public Services, 2001

38   Local Government Association, Local Authority Elections Factsheet, 2002

39   Data from the IdEA/Employers Organisation, National Census of Local Authority Councillors in England and Wales, 2001. The figures add up to 99.2% because 0.8% of councillors declined to answer.

40   Ibid.

41   Ibid.

42   Home Office, Community Cohesion, Report of the Independent Review Team, 2001

43   IdEA/Employers Organisation, op cit.

44   Employers' Organisation, Local Government Employment Survey, 2000

45   Ibid.

46   National Statistics, Labour Force Survey, 2001

47   Wilson and Game, op cit.

48   Ibid.

49   Labour Party, Renewing democracy, rebuilding communities, 1995

50   Paul Corrigan, No More Big Brother (Fabian Society Pamphlet), 1997

51   Ken Young and Nirmala Rao, Local Government Since 1945, 1997

52   Peter Latham, The Captive Local State (Spokesman Pamphlet), 2001

53   Labour Party, Because Britain Deserves Better, 1997

54   Margaret Hodge and Wendy Thompson, Beyond the Town Hall – re-inventing local government (Fabian Society Pamphlet), 1994

55   Hugh McConnel, Consumer-Responsive, Citizen-Remote, 1996 (University of Sheffield Political Economy Resource Centre Position Paper)

56   M.Loughlan, M.D. Gelfand and K.Young (eds), Half a Century of Municipal Decline 1935-1985, 1985

57   Jack Dromey, Geoffrey Filkin and Paul Corrigan, Modernising Local Government (Fabian Society Pamphlet), 1998

58   Ibid.

59   Martin Burch and Ian Holliday, 'New Labour and the machinery of government', in David Coates and Peter Lawler (eds), New Labour in power, 2000

60   Dave Sullivan and Andrew Stevens, 'The Progressive Council: The Case for Collaborative Local Politics', in Neal Lawson and Neil Sherlock (eds) The Progressive Century, 2000

61   Harold Laski, 'The committee system in local government', in A century of municipal progress: The last hundred years, 1935

62   Quoted in John Morrison, Reforming Britain, 2001

63   Ibid.

64   NOP for ITN Powerhouse programme, 28-30th Apr 2000.

65   'Steve Norris Gets Our Vote As A Capital Ambassador', Daily Express, 3 May 2000

66 Margaret Hodge, Steve Leach and Gerry Stoker, *More than the flower show: elected Mayors and democracy* (Fabian Society Pamphlet), 1997

67 Karen Day, *What Difference a Mayor Makes* (NLGN Pamphlet), 2000

68 Paul Simpson and Andrew Stevens, 'The Challenge for a Charismatic Local Democracy', in *Beyond Good Governance* (New Politics Network), 2000

69 DETR, *Modernising local government: Improving local services through Best Value*, 1998

70 Ibid.

71 Unison 'Positively Public' website www.unison.org.uk

72 Fred Robinson and Keith Shaw, *Who Runs the North East?*, 2001

73 DTLR, Local Public Service Agreements, 2001

74 James Plaskitt MP, 'Constitution', in Martin Linton, Katharine Raymond and Alan Whitehead (eds), *Beyond 2002*, 1999

75 Report of the Royal Commission on the Constitution, 1973

76 David Richards and Martin J. Smith, 'New Labour, the Constitution and Reforming the State', in Steve Ludlam and Martin J. Smith, *New Labour in Government*, 2001

77 DETR, *Building Partnerships for Prosperity*, 1998

78 Andrew Stevens, 'British exceptionalism' in *Soundings*, Summer 2002

79 Paul McQuail and Katy Donnelly, 'English Regional Government', in Robert Blackburn and Raymond Plant (eds), *Constitutional Reform*, 1999

80 Cabinet Office and DTLR, *Your Region, Your Choice*, 2002

81 Obtained from www.petermandelson.com/regions.shtml

82 Simon Partridge, *The British Union State*, (Catalyst Pamphlet 4), 1999

83 DETR, *Building Partnerships for Prosperity*, 1998, and Cabinet Office and DTLR, *Your Region, Your Choice*, 2002

84 See http://www.englishpm.demon.co.uk/case_against_regionalism.html

85 Ibid.

86 Localis Press Release, *Localis condemns regional proposals*, dated 9 May 2002

87 Denis Whelan, *Devolution All Round: A Manifesto for 2005*, 2002

88 Professor Alan Harding, *Is There a Missing Middle in English Governance?* (New Local Government Network), 2000

89 Briefing for the County Councils Network Regionalism Task Group, 1 March 2002

90 *Local Government Chronicle*, 16 November 2001, 'Prescott: regionalisation means reorganisation'

91 Cabinet Office and DTLR, 2002

92 Ibid.

93 Report of the Widdicombe Committee op. cit.

94 Geoffrey Filkin, Steve Dempsey, Andrew Larner and Greg Wilkinson, *Winning the e-revolution in local government* (New Local Government Network), 2001

95 Charles Leadbeater, *Living on Thin Air*, 2000

96 Geoffrey Filkin, Steve Dempsey, Andrew Larner and Greg Wilkinson op cit.

97 David Blunkett, *Politics and Progress*, 2001

98 Margaret Hodge and Wendy Thompson, 1994

99   Margaret Hodge, Steve Leach and Gerry Stoker, 1997
100   Malcolm Matson, *The last Rotten Borough* (Fabian Society Pamphlet), 1997
101   Andrew Adonis and Stephen Twigg, *The Cross We Bear: electoral reform for local government* (Fabian Society Pamphlet), 1997
102   John Whelan, 'Viagra time for Tory Local Government' in *The Reformer,* Autumn 1998
103   Steve Leach and Chris Game, Hung Authorities, *Elected Mayors and Cabinet Government* (Joseph Rowntree Foundation), 2000

Further reading

There are a multitude of good general local government books available and the best of these are listed here. For those seeking a more specialist enquiry the bibliographies contained in them should provide the reader with a handy reference point for the vast expanse of topical literature, political pamphlets, government papers, case studies and academic research papers that exists out there.

General

T.Byrne (2000), *Local Government in Britain* (7th ed), Penguin

H.Elcock (1994), *Local Government: Policy and Management in Local Authorities* (3rd ed), Routledge

R.Fenney (2002), *Essential Local Government* (10th ed), LGC/National Council for the Training of Journalists

P.W.Jackson (1970), *Local Government*, Butterworths

G.Jones and J.Stewart (1985), T*he Case for Local Government*, George Allen & Unwin

J.Kingdom (1991), *Local Government and Politics in Britain*, Philip Allan

R.Leach and J.Percy-Smith (2001), *Local Governance in Britain*, Palgrave

P.G.Richards (1983), *The Local Government System*, George Allen & Unwin

J.Stanyer (1976), *Understanding Local Government*, Fontana

D.Wilson and C.Game (1998), *Local Government in the United Kingdom* (2nd ed), Macmillan

The History of Local Government

W.I.Jennings, H.Laski and W.A.Robson (1935), A *century of municipal progress: The last hundred years*, George Allen and Unwin

M.Loughlan, M.D. Gelfand and K.Young (eds) (1985), *Half a Century of Municipal Decline 1935-1985*, George Allen & Unwin

B.Lucas and P.G.Richards (1978), *A History of Local Government in the Twentieth Century*, George Allen & Unwin

C.W.Pearce (1980), *The Machinery of Change in Local Government 1888-1974*, George Allen & Unwin

J.Redlich and F.W.Hirst (1970), *Local Government in England*, Macmillan

K.Young and N.Rao (1997), *Local Government since 1945*, Blackwell

Local Government Theory

C.Cockburn (1977), *The Local State: management of cities and people*, Pluto Press

S.Duncan and M.Goodwin (1988), *The Local State and Uneven Development*, Polity

D.Hill (1974), *Democratic Theory and Local Government*, George Allen & Unwin
D.M.Hill (2000), *Urban policy and politics in Britain*, Macmillan
Sir I.Jennings, *Principles of Local Government Law*, 1965
M.Loughlin (1986), *Local Government in the Modern State*, Sweet and Maxwell
W.J.M.McKenzie (1961), *Theories of Local Government*, LSE
N.Rao (1994), *The Making and Un-making of Local Self-government*, Dartmouth

Management
J.Barrett (1988), *Organising for Local Government*, Longman
D.Farnham and S.Horton (1996), *Managing the New Public Services*, Macmillan
A.Griffiths (1989), *Local Government Administration*, Shaw
R.Knowles (1985), *Effective Management in Local Government*, ICSA
R.S.B.Knowles (1987), *The Law and Practice of Local Authority Meetings*, ICSA
S.Leach, J.Stewart and K.Walsh (1994), *The Changing Organisation and Management of Local Government*, Macmillan
J.Stewart (1986), *The New Management of Local Government*, George Allen & Unwin
K.Walsh (1984), *Ethics and the Local Government Officer*, INLOGOV

The Politics of Local Government
A.Alexander (1982), *The Politics of Local Government in the United Kingdom*, Longman
D.Blunkett and G.Green (1983), *Building from the Bottom: The Sheffield Experience*, Fabian Society
D.Blunkett and K.Jackson (1987), *Democracy in Crisis: The Town Halls Respond*, Hogarth
M.Boddy and C.Fudge (1984), *Local Socialism*, Macmillan
P.Dunleavy (1980), *Urban Political Analysis*, Macmillan
J.Gibson (1990), *The Politics and Economics of the Poll Tax: Mrs Thatcher's downfall*, EMAS
N.Flynn, S.Leach and C.Vielba (1985), *Abolition or Reform? The GLC and the Metropolitan County Councils*, George Allen & Unwin
W.Grant (1977), *Independent local politics in England and Wales*, Saxon House
J.Gyford (1985), *The politics of Local Socialism*
J.Gyford et al (1989), *The Changing Politics of Local Government*, Unwin Hyman
W.Hampton (1991), *Local Government and Urban Politics*, Longman
P. Houlihan (1986), *Politics of Local Government*, Longman
S.Lansley, S.Goss and C.Wolmar (1989), *Councils in Conflict: The Rise and Fall of the Municipal Left*, Macmillan
N.Ridley (1988), *The Local Right: enabling not providing*, Centre for Policy Studies
G.Stoker (1991), *The Politics of Local Government*, Macmillan
G.Stoker (ed) (2000), *The New Politics of British Local Governance*, Macmillan

Local Government Finance
S.Bailey (1999), *Local Government Economics*, Macmillan

W.Birtles and A.Forge (1999), *Butterworth's Local Government Finance*, Butterworth

N.P.Hepworth (1984), *The Finance of Local Government*, George Allen & Unwin

K.Newton and T.J.Karran (1985), *The Politics of Local Expenditure*, Macmillan

T.Travers (1989), *The Politics of Local Government Finance*, George Allen & Unwin

London Governance

M.D'Arcy and R.MacLean (2000), *Nightmare!*, Politico's

M.Herbert and T.Travers (1988), *The London Government Handbook*, Cassell

S.Inwood (1998), *A History of London*, Macmillan

P.Hall (1980), *Radical Agenda for London*, Fabian Society

M.Matson (1997), *The last Rotten Borough*, Fabian Society

B.Pimlott and N.Rao (2002), *Governing London*, Oxford University Press

R.Porter (2000), *London: A Social History*, Penguin

Dame S.Porter (1990), *A Minister for London: A Capital Concept*, FPL Financial

G.Rhodes and G.R.Ruck (1970), *The Government of Greater London*, George Allen & Unwin

A.Saint (ed) (1989), *Politics and the People of London*, Hambledon Press

T.Travers (1991), *The government of London*, LSE

T.Travers and G.Jones (1997), *The new government of London*, JRF

W.Whitehouse (2000), *GLC – The Inside Story*, James Lester

Local Government and New Labour

A.Adonis and Twigg, S. (1997), *The Cross We Bear: electoral reform for local government*, Fabian Society

H.Atkinson and S.Wilks-Heeg (2000), *Local Government from Thatcher to Blair*, Polity

T.Blair (1998), *Leading the way: A new vision for local government*, IPPR

P.Corrigan (1997), *No More Big Brother*, Fabian Society

D.Coates and P.Lawler (eds) (2000), *New Labour in power*, Manchester University Press

J.Dromey, G.Filkin and P.Corrigan (1998), *Modernising Local Government*, Fabian Society

M.Hodge and W.Thompson (1994), *Beyond the Town Hall – re-inventing local government*, Fabian Society

M.Hodge, S.Leach and G.Stoker (1997), *More than the flower show: elected Mayors and democracy*, Fabian Society

P.Latham (2001), *The Captive Local State*, Spokesman

S.Leach and D.Wilson (2000), *Local Political Leadership*, Policy Press

J.Newman (2001), *Modernising Governance*, Sage

N.Rao (2000), *Reviving Local Democracy*, Policy Press

A.Seldon (ed) (2001), *The Blair Effect*, Little, Brown and Co.

Index

Index